CURVEBALL

CURVEBALL

When Your Faith Takes Turns You Never Saw Coming
(or, How I Stumbled and Tripped My Way
to Finding a Bigger God)

PETER ENNS

HarperOne
An Imprint of HarperCollinsPublishers

FIRST EDITION

Designed by Terry McGrath

Library of Congress Cataloging-in-Publication Data has been applied for.

ISBN 978-0-06-309347-8

23 24 25 26 27 LBC 5 4 3 2 1

For Beau James
(aka Beau Beaus, Beau Buddy, Little Guy)
b. November 19, 2019
When you grow up I hope you will read
(or at least buy) all my books.
And thank you for believing in me.
Grandpa loves you very much.

Neither do people pour new wine into old wineskins. If they
do, the skins will burst; the wine will run out and the wineskins
will be ruined. No, they pour new wine into new wineskins, and
both are preserved.

—Matthew 9:17 (NIV)

The whole world before you is like a speck that tips the scales,
        and like a drop of morning dew that falls on the ground.
But you are merciful to all, for you can do all things,
        and you overlook people's sins, so that they may repent.
For you love all things that exist,
        and detest none of the things that you have made,
        for you would not have made anything if you had hated it.
How would anything have endured if you had not willed it?
Or how would anything not called forth by you have been preserved?
You spare all things, for they are yours, O Lord, you who love the living.
For your immortal spirit is in all things.

—Wisdom 11:22-12:1 (NIV)

The cosmos is an ocean that drowns every mind.

—Nicodemus of the Holy Mountain

Contents

Abundant Life

I spent much of my life unknowingly abdicating the task of taking full responsibility for my faith. In my younger years, I largely accepted and absorbed the narrative of faith that had been written for me, thinking it to be my own. Then for two decades, as I was busy working and parenting, I would occasionally tweak the surface of it—I guess I was too preoccupied for anything other than some light editing for punctuation and typos.

And so later in life, when moments of spiritual reckoning demanded more of me, I was ill prepared.

Life, it turns out, has a habit of throwing us curveballs. By curveball, I don't mean some bump in the road that could easily have been avoided, nor some annoyingly uncomfortable moment that can be handled by distracting ourselves on our phones, going for a jog, or flipping channels. I mean those experiences that are so momentous we simply cannot continue living as if they hadn't happened—everything changes, and we know we cannot remain as we were.

As for me, my inherited beliefs eventually ran out of steam and collapsed in on themselves. They could no longer explain my day-to-day experiences and, rather, always seemed to be at odds with them. This led to a dark and difficult period in my life of not knowing what to believe, if anything. And if my decades of teaching, speaking, and writing count for anything, I am hardly the first or only person with a story like that.

These upending experiences can be deeply personal and, as in my case, literally cosmic. But whatever they are, they have a habit of boring deep into the very foundations of our stories and calling into question the validity of core elements of the story. Once that happens, the story needs a Part Two—an after.

The big lesson I learned from wrestling with my own curveballs is how deeply my faith in God had been cemented in fear—which is to say, how I viewed God as very much antagonistic toward me. And so any thought on my part of listening to my experiences and interrogating my inherited faith—to inspect its boundaries let alone climb over its walls—was seen as a crisis that had to be averted or at least resolved immediately.

But over time I would come to see that this is precisely the wrong attitude to take. This fear-crisis model of faith, where all things had to fall into place "or else," was simply no match for my raw, complex, messy, out-of-control existence. And this got me thinking differently about God. If the infinite God of the cosmos is real, surely God understands my puny humanity and sees my questions and struggles as more than a nuisance. It would take years for me to truly accept the idea that *my disruptive experiences are not outside impositions to or an attack on my faith, but are the soil out of which my faith matures and takes shape.* The thought of ignoring what my head and heart were screaming at me and simply staying the course became not only more and more difficult, but—if God is truly real—utterly nonsensical. Can I really "ignore my experiences"? Can any of us? Is this really what God expects of us? If we ignore them, then what is left of "us"?

This realization was the game-changer. It created a space for me to step away from the fear-crisis model of faith and toward a curious-hopeful model. That model is built on seeing God as a relentless, compassionate inner presence in my life, always beckoning me forward. That model is one of peace, curiosity, and hopefulness and rests on my embrace of the mystery and love of God.

I value the experiences of my younger years—they are still part of my story. I am still a Christian but a different sort of Christian than before. I am not one driven by fear of slipping off the tightrope with the next stiff wind. Rather, I am seeking to live into the sacred space of God's Presence with curiosity, hope, peace, and love of others. I believe this is the type of relationship God seeks to have with us.

I continue writing my narrative, of course—as are we all. We are dealing, after all, with the infinite Creator of the infinite cosmos, so how can it be otherwise? Working out faith "on the go," as it were, is very good news, indeed. I can live my life seeking God with curiosity, courage, security, and peace, knowing that making adjustments is a part of the life of faith.

Jesus said, "The thief comes only to steal and kill and destroy. I came that they may have life, and have it abundantly" (John 10:10). An abundant faith while embracing the curveballs of life—that's what I'm after, and that's what this book is all about.

Chapter 1

My True Purpose. Or Not.

A T THE AGE OF NINE I found my true purpose in life—to play major league baseball. I'd been smitten with the baseball bug while flipping channels and landing on WPIX 11 in New York City, the station that carried Yankees games. I still have a memory of those innocent black-and-white images. My parents were German immigrants who knew nothing of baseball, so it came to me as something of a spiritual epiphany rather than an heirloom. To this day I thank my lucky stars for this formative moment (and that I didn't stop at WOR 9 and become a Mets fan).

Now, spoiler alert—I did not become a professional baseball player. So why am I still thanking my lucky stars? Because you never outgrow your childhood passions—and if you're lucky, you get to bring them back into your life in ways you couldn't have predicted when you were all-or-nothing convinced of what you would and wouldn't do when you grew up. To quote Terence Mann (played by James Earl Jones in *Field of Dreams*), "The one constant for me through the years has been baseball"—through all the twists and turns and ups and downs, for longer than I've been a husband, a parent, a professor, or a Christian, giving me delight and, like most things worthwhile, frustration.* To this day, forty years after I had to stop playing, I still find myself randomly picking up a bat I keep near my desk and giving it a few swings (hey dogs, move!), holding a baseball in my old pitching hand or putting an old glove up to my face and breathing in the still lingering scent of leather and glove oil.

God, however—well, that's another thing. God has been a part of my life journey, too, as far as I can remember, but in a more complicated way. To be honest, God has never felt as dependable as the rhythms of baseball and has often proved more frustrating. At least in baseball you have some predictability, some consistency, some clear and unimpeachable boundaries. Three strikes and you're out, three outs a side, and the team with the most runs wins.

But, as I would come to find out, God doesn't seem to have *any* predictability, consistency, or clearly defined structure, despite what I had been taught to think. In a crushing disappointment in my young life, I experienced how I could not count on God, even though "counting on God to come through" was what my church had taught me with as much uncompromising clarity as "a ball that goes over the fence is a home run."

So when, as a recent college graduate, my young life arrived at a moment of truth, I was sure that God had been leading me to my deepest desire. I was resting on the invariable, Newtonian-like law, as sure as gravity, that God is fair, grants us the true and pure longings of our hearts, and is faithful to us as we are faithful to Him.** But at that precise moment, God was AWOL when some stupid, random thing intervened to thwart my life's purpose, shortchange my future—and blow up my faith and my world.

---

* As for frustration, hey Yankees fans, remember 2001 and 2004? Have you recovered yet? Because I haven't.

** At that time I thought God was gendered, but I no longer think this way. My thinking of God has grown on that point, and, as you will see, on several others.

I thought God behaved a certain way. I found out God doesn't. So now what would I do?

My First Blown Elbow

But back to when everything was still in place before it came apart.

Months after my television epiphany, I started playing Little League baseball, which immediately became the purest source of joy of my childhood. I was obsessed. On game days—in a scene straight out of *The Wonder Years*—I would hop on my metallic green Schwinn Sting-Ray and get to the field an hour before we were supposed to. I just sat in the dugout. Alone. My happy place. Pete Rose famously said he would walk through hell in a gasoline suit just to play baseball. Fine, Pete, but would you do it an hour early? Hmm? I don't think so. Anyway, just putting on my old-school flannel uniform and pulling up my stirrup socks made my stomach flutter.

A rained-out game was more devastating to me than the flood was to Noah's generation. In fact, one particular rainout led me, at the age of eleven, to my first act of blasphemy, at least the first one I remember. It had rained all day, and by late afternoon the game was cancelled. As if on cue, no sooner was the game called than *the clouds parted, and the sun shone warm and bright,* as if to mock me. I was was SO ANGRY I looked up at the sky and spit out the words, "Damn you." I'm not kidding. I was eleven and I damned God. Nothing I've ever written about God that has made my critics go nuts can even come close to this sacrilegious moment of biblical proportions.

You get the picture: I. Loved. Playing. Baseball. There was never a single moment when my interest waned. I wanted to play all the time and planned on doing so until I was too old and they had to cart me off the field in an iron lung. And like countless kids the world over, I wanted to one day play in the major leagues, and anyone who tried to lecture me with a dose of its statistical unlikelihood became immediately dead to me.

Memories tend to bend and twist in our favor as we recall them, but I am not far off the mark when I say that I got to be a pretty good ball player. I could always throw hard, so as I got older I gravitated toward pitching. During college summers I played on a semi-pro team, and as a college senior, I was nationally ranked among Division III pitchers in "strikeouts per nine innings."[1] Some scouts came to watch me pitch. Playing professional baseball was becoming a distinct possibility. I wasn't a top prospect, but I was good and wanted a chance. If I could just get their attention, get my foot in the door, I *knew*, with God's help, I could make it.

One week after my college career ended I was home working out with my semi-pro team. I was already scheduled to go to several tryout camps over the next few weeks, one of them at Shea Stadium in New York where the Mets played at the time. My coach encouraged me to work on a pitch that most professionals have in their arsenal, a slider, which is like a curveball but is thrown much faster and curves at a sharper angle. It also puts a lot of stress on the elbow.

After about fifteen minutes I was starting to get a feel for how to use this new weapon—until I felt a pop and burning sensation in my elbow. I went home to ice it, as was my routine, but after forty-five minutes with the elbow in a bucket, the pain was just as bad. That had never happened before. I knew I had a problem, but I didn't yet know how severe. It would take me a few weeks to realize that my baseball dream ended that afternoon.

The diagnosis (without the benefit of MRIs) was tendonitis, and the recommendation was several weeks of rest. But I didn't have several weeks. My window WAS the next several weeks. So, with tryouts looming, I spent the summer frantically praying and rehabbing like I was bailing water out of a sinking canoe, icing constantly, and showing up at tryouts smelling of Ben-Gay. At times my arm hurt so bad I could barely comb my hair. Each day I waited for God to show up to bring me some miraculous healing.

The best shot I had was the Shea Stadium tryout in July of that year. My arm had calmed down enough to make a go of it, and I impressed the scouts—one even said "whoa!" after I uncorked my first fastball. Maybe this is actually happening? After I got done, I turned to them and could see they liked what they saw. They clearly did . . . until one of the scouts asked me my age. "Twenty-one." Without a word—not a single word—they both turned and walked away. Conversation over. Apparently twenty-one was too old.[2] I was stunned. What just happened?! My life's dream was being swept away like crumbs off a kitchen counter.

I lingered in the locker room long after the other guys had left, hoping to catch a private moment with one of the scouts to see what I could do to persuade them to sign me. I don't recall the conversation, but whatever I said made no difference. All I remember is driving back home across the George Washington Bridge to New Jersey in the denial stage of grief.

I hung on for a few weeks that summer, still pasting my arm together as best as I could for some other tryouts. But by the end of August, I was tired of the pain and tired of the uphill climb against the odds. With mourning, I put my glove and spikes aside and moved on.

That's when my baseball journey ended. And that's when my real journey began, a journey I am still on long after baseball went back to something I watched rather than did.

I thought God behaved a certain way. I found out God doesn't. So, where would that leave me? What am I supposed to think about God? What exactly *is* "God" anyway? Those questions were no longer academic. They would shape my journey of faith for the rest of my life, long after this blown elbow healed and others would come.

Oh Lord, Thanks for Nothing

Baseball was the trial of my youth and young adulthood, but I know it's just a game. My pain and disappointment are not to be compared to the hardships and devastations others face throughout the world at any moment and across time. But I don't feel the need to rank pain. For me, at that moment, this was my crisis and therefore my entry point to a path I had never walked, one where my lifelong baseball dream incinerated along with my understanding of God.

Some of my ideas about God were shaped by my parents. God and Jesus were real, but I didn't have much content beyond that. There were no family Bible readings or prayer times, apart from a traditional German prayer before dinner. In junior high school, my parents did send my sister and me to a Lutheran church for two years of confirmation classes. I remember memorizing the Nicene Creed, and the changing festive colors that marked the church calendar. But I never really internalized any of that until a few years later, near the end of my sophomore year of high school, when my religious life took a life-changing turn.

It was the mid-1970s and I found myself in a jam-packed small church that was attracting the younger crowd seeking meaning in life. I had never seen a church like that—a lively place with electric guitars, drums, and a lot of laughter. For several months beforehand, I had had what I still believe are some real, tangible experiences of God. I actually felt hounded by God while walking the halls in my high school or strolling the aisles at the supermarket. I felt that day in church was decision time, the moment God had been leading me toward. I gave in to the "hound of heaven," from a late-nineteenth-century poem by Francis Thompson, raised my hand (with "every head bowed and every eye closed"), and, in the language of the day, "accepted Jesus into my heart."

For the next six years—through high school, college, and that post-college summer of baseball trauma—this was my church. I owe it a lot, but it focused almost exclusively on getting people to convert, which left little room for getting into deeper questions. The content of faith was considered to be fairly straightforward: God's relationship with humans was basically transactional. Humans sin and God punishes sinners—God *has* to because He hates sin so much. But Jesus stepped in and took the punishment for us. Our side of the transaction, our only obligation, was to accept that Jesus did this—and really mean it—so that when we die, we go to heaven rather than burn in hell for eternity.

Meantime, while we are waiting either to die or for Jesus's Second Coming (which could literally happen at any second), we had to work very hard to make sure we lived lives worthy of people who have Jesus in their hearts. If not, our conversion would fly out the window, leaving us once again on the outside, like our forebears Adam and Eve, who, having tasted paradise, were nevertheless tossed out, with angels brandishing flaming swords barring any hope of reentrance.

I bought in to staying the course, confident that God would be with me every step of the way, keeping me safe, answering my prayers, and helping me become a bold, confident disciple. That's what I was taught, or at least what I caught, and it was reinforced by a steady diet of Contemporary Christian Music and other entrapments of conservative evangelical Christian culture.

Because I was an intellectually curious person, some of the pieces never quite came together for me. About a year after my conversion, that initial excitement began to wane, and I started having questions about the logic of this or that church teaching. But the only way the church equipped me to deal with doubts was to raise my hand and get saved again, seeing as the first one didn't seem to take. And that made me even more motivated, probably more so subconsciously, to do things that I felt would make God very pleased with me, like trying to drag my friends to church (which never worked—sorry, guys!), reading my Bible daily, listening to mainly Christian music, and laying before God my deepest desires so that He would take over, see them through, and all the glory could be to Him.

But my deepest desire melted like summer snow when my elbow popped and those scouts about-faced me in Shea Stadium.

My baseball dream and my faith that gave my life structure, meaning, and security about the future crashed into a three-foot-thick block of concrete at sixty miles an hour. All I could do was sit there in the middle of the road shaken, stunned, wondering whether this had really happened. I couldn't explain it all away. I couldn't make up good excuses for God. Doubt and disillusionment were beginning to take root, along with resentment, anger, and most of all just plain sadness. My elbow popped, and God was a no-show. Now what?

Adjusting My Swing

I look back now, forty years later, and can say that I believe God is nothing at all like the deity I had given up on—quite the opposite, in fact. But at the time, the nice, down-the-middle batting-practice, grapefruit-sized, easy-to-hit pitch that my faith had led me to expect from God suddenly and fiercely curved down and away from me in mid-swing. Life had thrown me my first curveball. I never saw it coming. Strike three, three outs, game over.

We all face our own curveballs. Something happens—small or great, out of the ordinary and wholly unexpected—that makes us question what we've always believed about God, and what our next move should be.

It was two full years before the sadness of a crushed dream gave way to some peace. But for me to get there, my understanding of God had to be adjusted from the man upstairs who grants wishes to another kind of God—one who sees my pain, understands it, sits with me in it, and then walks with me along the slow and steady path of inside-out transformation because of it. It took time, and I would like nothing more than to be able to package a three-step formula for others to follow, but, of course, faith in the infinite God doesn't work that way. Eventually, however, my faith shifted from despair to something deeper, more textured, more real, more complicated—more grown up.

When we get thrown a curveball, it doesn't have to mean "game over," but it does mean we have to be willing to make adjustments to our swing in order to make contact with the ball. As Hall of Famer Willie Stargell said, "To me, baseball has always been a reflection of life. Like life, it adjusts. It survives everything." Yay, Willie! But let me add that baseball does more than survive—it thrives, it grows, it evolves. The same can be said for faith.

My faith crisis was not about God as much as it was about how I expected God to show up. That is the big lesson I learned during that season of my life, and would come to learn in deeper ways as the decades of my life passed. My blown elbow experience came to be a signpost writ large not that God wasn't real (though I definitely had my periods of serious doubt); rather, I came to understand that *my understanding of God* was not adequate for handling reality. My crushed dream was an invitation—actually, an offer I couldn't refuse—to recognize that I had been laboring under a small view of God. I was beginning to find out that God is bigger, completely out of my control, and more mysterious than I had been able to capture in slogans and childish expectations.

Making adjustments to how we think about God and faith isn't easy, at least I can say so for myself. But I can recall two small steps I began taking in those early post-college years that helped me inch forward when all I knew about God was falling apart.

First, processing with people I trusted was huge—even if their experiences didn't match mine exactly. Some of my friends had grown a little skeptical of their inherited faith, too. I can't say we always handled our newfound skepticism with insight and maturity—we spent way too much time poking fun at the low-hanging fruit of TV preachers. (If you're up for it, please do type "Tootin' Tilton" into your search engine.) But still, I had some friends who were on a similar journey, and I needed that camaraderie in my life. Finding a new, if also small, community that embraced curiosity was key.

Second, I expanded my community another way, by reading books to help me grasp a vision for Christian faith that understood God differently from what I had been exposed to. That alone was a bit of a miracle, since I wasn't much of a reader back in those days. But because I sensed this deep need to learn, I started reading anything I could get my hands on: theology, biblical interpretation, church history, philosophy, not to mention C. S. Lewis's *The Chronicles of Narnia*, which gave me a sense of how faith needs our imagination—a necessary tool for experiencing the mystery of God, as I would come to see years later.

I may not have understood the full implications of everything I read in those books, but they became an extended community across time. They gave me much needed perspective and helped affirm that my desire to seek a bigger God wasn't a sign that I was going crazy.

These two steps—expanded community and growing in knowledge—would become part of my stride of faith for the rest of my life. Not that they provided final answers to my questions, but they set me on a path that let me experience God differently—a path that has continued and broadened throughout my life. Today, I would express myself very differently, but that is exactly the point: my understanding of God has continued to change because the curveballs and the adjustments did not stop coming. I'm just thankful that early on I came to see that it was fine and good to make adjustments to how I understood God.

And it is never too late in life to make those adjustments.

Don't Be Afraid

This book is about our faith in God and what can happen when what we thought we knew about God is confronted by everyday experiences that challenge, upset, and refuse to align with that faith. What happens next? What do we *do*?

Rather than telling you how you should respond to your curveballs, I'd like to relate a bit of how I have responded to mine. I've had many experiences, utterly unscripted, that I could not ignore over the years and that have put me in a place to see God differently. I cannot tell you what steps you should take to move forward, but I would like to encourage you to become more aware of that inner voice telling you that adjustments are needed *and* not to feel broken or unfaithful about making those adjustments. I guarantee you are walking a common path.

But I am also hoping to channel a sense of urgency. Interrogating our ideas about God is vital for a healthy faith in the world we live in. When our understanding of God is etched in granite and kept behind a glass case, never to be touched, we are not being faithful—we are actually undermining the continued viability of our faith. My own faith has been enriched and deepened by adjusting my *limited* understanding of God to address some of the more pressing questions that have arisen for me, questions about the Bible, science, life and death, and other things. Had I not done so, I don't think I could have continued on my faith journey at all.

Adjustments are good. Adjustments are inevitable. Adjustments are evidence of a growing faith.

I am not interested here in defending how our experiences prove (or disprove) God. Rather, I want to show how my experiences have called me to see a God beyond the limiting and inadequate conceptions of God I had. My ultimate hope for you is that you will find something here that will help you come to find a "better" God as you handle whatever curveballs you face. When I cursed God at age eleven, I was cursing a false deity. When I gave up on the God of my baseball dream, I gave up on a codependent deity invested in making sure that Pete's plan for Pete's life would happen just the way Pete wanted it to in order to keep Pete from having bad feelings.

I would come to know more blown elbows in the years to come, more curveballs that led (or shoved) me to look deep inside and interrogate my understanding of God, where it fell short, and to make adjustments. And all of my adjustments eventually—sometimes with great difficulty—led me further into landscapes of faith I would otherwise have never seen. I was learning to leave a fear-crisis model of faith and move toward a curious-hopeful model.

We will always have to face our curveballs about God because our understanding of the limitless God is always limited, partial, in need of revision. We never arrive at a place where adjustments are no longer necessary, where our human limitations have been overcome. Adjusting our understanding of God isn't a sign of weak faith, nor is it an attack on faith—it *is* faith.

The curveballs in our lives are where the real growth happens. In that sense they are blessed moments, visions of grace. I don't say that lightly. I am not suggesting that in the face of grievous darkness we put on a smiley face because "God has a plan" (yuk). The circumstances that bring us to face our small understanding of God are marked by real loss and pain that will come to us in varying intensities and durations.

But after the loss and pain—indeed, *because* we have experienced loss and pain—we may also catch glimpses of a grander vision of God, where God is beyond our control; beyond the inadequate convictions that carried us through in earlier seasons; beyond the claims of absolute, unquestioned religious formulations; beyond any limitations we place on God, intentionally or not—a God whose ways, to echo Paul, are inscrutable and whose mind cannot be known, a God who surpasses all understanding. Our job in all this is to try to be willing to stay awake to what our experiences are telling us about this better God and to make adjustments when necessary.

Ironically, the big obstacle that got in the way of my doing just that was my own religious tradition. So that is where we begin.

Chapter 2

I Love You, Bible.
Just Not "That" Way.

I T WAS AN OCTOBER AFTERNOON in 1989, and I was in my first semester of doctoral studies. I remember that day because that's when
it all began falling apart.

After a day of classes, I rode my ten-speed back home to our little
apartment, parked it out back, and walked into the kitchen as always.
But today would be different. Today I would have a conversation with
the refrigerator.

All I remember clearly is standing there staring at the Maytag and
uttering a thought that I had been suppressing for weeks but that was
now ready to spew forth: "I don't know if Abraham was a real person.
I . . . don't think he was. Most of Genesis, in fact, seems more like
stories than history."

There. I said it. Finally.

I wasn't exactly expecting an answer from the freezer compartment,
but within 0.4 seconds, another voice I had been keeping at bay for
weeks, a voice of judgment, elbowed its way to the front: "Abraham?
The father of Israel? *Never lived?!* Uh oh, you're in TROU-OU-BLE

with God now! And wait till everyone hears how you've gone full-on heretical in four weeks. Nice work. What a weak-minded joke you are. Shame on you."

As this dialogue was happening, my wife and our firstborn were playing in the next room. The joyful sights and sounds of normal life and my unexpected theological crisis were coexisting, occupying the same time and space, and both were undeniably real. From that moment on, wrestling with unsettling thoughts about the Bible would be as much a part of my normal routine as feeding and changing our two-year-old son.

I had always been taught that the Bible is our main and best guide for understanding what God was all about. My curveball here was watching my study of the Bible cause that view of the Bible—and the God who stood behind it—to slip away from me. And this wasn't simply an intellectual exercise. That voice of judgment in my head mirrored my community of faith. I had a lot to lose.

Be Careful What You Wish For

Looking at this on a larger scale, that moment was my first real confrontation with an age-old problem—whether sacred texts should be read literally or whether they are best read figuratively or symbolically. That question is as old as Christianity and Judaism but has blown up in recent generations because of the impact of science and the modern study of history. Not only have Judaism and Christianity had to address this problem, but so have Islam and any other religious traditions with an ancient sacred text that is understood to lay a claim on our modern lives. I was never entirely oblivious to this issue, but I was always able to keep it at a safe distance—until that moment facing the Maytag.

What made the question so urgent for me is the following factoid that religious groups with sacred texts tend to believe: God was in some way personally and directly responsible for producing those texts. God inspired human authors to write every word God wanted written, in exacting detail, which is why—speaking for my own tradition—the Bible is often called the "word of God."

Now here is the real twist. In the Protestant circles I had been moving in for half my life at that time, a God-inspired text had serious implications. Among them, perhaps the most important, is that the Bible, as the word of God, can clearly never be wrong about anything, and in particular about history. And that's what prompted my Maytag moment: by confessing that I was no longer sure that father Abraham ever existed, I had willingly and knowingly crossed a tightly guarded boundary.

Few things raise the alarm quicker for biblical literalists than saying the Bible has historical problems. Over time, I would learn to turn down the dial on that inner voice of judgment and shame, though it was difficult and my wrestling still bubbles to the surface now and then. After all, the dire consequences of betraying my Jedi training and going over to the dark side had been drilled deep into my evangelical marrow for many years. Whenever a threatening thought dared to enter my mind, a scolding auto response was programmed to kick in <cue deep, throaty Darth Vader breathing>: *God finds your lack of faith . . . disturbing. After all, He sent His only Son to die for you on the cross, and this is the thanks He gets?! You can't even keep it together for Him and just believe the Bible like everybody else? More than disappointed—God is now actually about-face angry with you, Pete. If you don't repent of your weak-spined faith, right yourself, and return to the fold quickly, you will continue zip-lining down the slope to total unbelief and the pit of eternal fire waiting for people like you.*

And yet (if I may think out loud for a moment), was this scenario really my fault? If my notions about the Bible could evaporate like an August dew within a half-semester of doctoral classes and doing some reading, then perhaps the weakness wasn't in my spine. Like a frail plant that needs careful tending and constant protection from sun and wind, perhaps the real problem wasn't me but the fragile, unsustainable version of Christianity I had been told was my only option. Maybe the pressure of reading the Bible "literally or else" was the deeper problem, not my questioning it.

To continue with my Maytag moment, I had just graduated from seminary five months earlier—a seminary I would describe as thoughtful though staunchly conservative. I entered seminary never having had any serious thoughts about becoming a pastor (because, eww, people). I just had a drive to learn all I could about the God I said I believed in, and, as a good Protestant, that meant studying the Bible.

Thanks to my professors, seminary kick-started in me a love for exploring the sacred text. I liked it so much that I decided to go to graduate school to focus on the Hebrew Bible—what Christians usually call the Old Testament. After all, that part of the Christian Bible is famously difficult for keeping a Christian's interest, with all of its begats, conflicts with science, strange laws, repetitive stories of corrupt kings, and prophets going on for pages about Neo-Assyrians. But it also happens to make up about three-quarters of the Christian Bible. Sooner or later I knew I'd have to deal with it, so I might as well dive in, grab that tiger by the tail, and put the pedal to the metal. So, in the late summer of 1989, my young family and I made the trek from the land of the Phillies (ew) to the land of the Red Sox (more ew) and Harvard University's Department of Near Eastern Languages and Civilizations. I couldn't wait! I hit the ground with wheels spinning at eighty miles per hour.

Had I known the emotional cost that journey would demand of me (personally and socially), I might have slunk back into the waiting arms of a familiar faith, where the Bible is not seriously questioned, let alone interrogated. To be completely honest, even during my seminary years, I was always a little skeptical about a view of the Bible where all the pieces aligned like metal filings under a magnet. But I did not comprehend how profoundly my experiences in the next five years would change me, and would continue to for decades to come and to the present day.

Over the years, I would do a lot of blank staring amid existential crises—while riding on public transportation or shopping for groceries, during parent-teacher nights and in-law visits, during sermons (even my own), and at other times when a fifteen-second stare off into space is socially awkward. But, to jump ahead a bit, I now view those early experiences, difficult though they were, as moments of God's Presence that would lead to much needed personal transformation.

I would later come to see that on that fall day in front of the fridge, I was taking my first real steps toward what Jesus called dying to yourself—and yes, dying to ourselves often means dying to our understanding of God. I was beginning a slow process of learning to interrogate not so much the Bible but my unexamined beliefs *about* the Bible, which were baked into me more deeply than I knew, and—this is the real point—affected directly *how I thought about God.* If left unchecked, that path would have certainly derailed me as life became more complex in the years to come.

The Beatles and Israelite Origins

Have you ever believed something to be absolutely true only to find that the truth is more complicated? Like the Beatles?

In my early teen imagination, I was the fifth Beatle—or simply George's replacement. I idolized them, those innocent, happy-go-lucky, mop top Liverpudlians who effortlessly wrote globally catchy tunes as easily as most mortals flick on a light switch. But over time the fantasy took a big hit. I came to realize they were complex mortals, had troubled marriages, and sometimes weren't nice people to be around. In order to stay on the Beatles train, I had to accept who they in fact were and allow that new knowledge to bring me to a more realistic— and eventually deeper—appreciation for their music.

My changing relationship with the Bible during my doctoral program was something like that. If you will allow a few paragraphs of toned-down nerdiness, here's what happened.

A main focus of Hebrew Bible doctoral programs in research universities is "Israelite origins"—the historical study of how the ancient Israelites emerged onto the world scene at the beginning of the Iron Age (around 1200 BCE, two hundred years before King David). As a historical course of study, the focus of these programs is on archaeological and linguistic evidence along with a close reading of the Hebrew Bible. This approach has a name: "historical criticism"—*historical* because the goal is to understand Israel's beginnings, and *critical* because you're not just going to take the Bible's word to tell you what happened back then.

On that second point, I may have lost some of you ("whaddayamean you can't take the Bible's word for it?"), but hang with me. The thing is, the Hebrew Bible was written by, and for, Israelites, who had skin in the game. These ancient authors weren't deceptive, but they weren't detached and objective, either. They were writing for the benefit of their own communities. Lessons needed to be learned, faces needed to be saved, and enemies needed to be rhetorically put in their place. Since the authors had a vested interest in what was said and how it was said, agendas and biases could hardly be kept out. Actually, agendas and biases were the point. This is true not only of the Bible but of any ancient writers' accounts of their own history.

In theory, that shouldn't sound too strange. Think of the story of the triumphant American experience, the one that past generations (including my own) learned in school. As it turns out, the story I was taught was biased. It left out vital parts, like the treatment of indigenous peoples, the true horrors of slavery, systemic racism, the injustice of generational poverty, and the greedy exploitation of resources by the rich and powerful.

All history writing has some bias, and it's not always intentional. As humans, we just have filters through which we see our world. But sometimes the bias *is* intentional when parts of the past are ignored, skewed, or distorted by those who have the power to control the narrative. Only in recent decades have the dominant narratives of the American experience been scrutinized for their spin. Think, for example, of the American controversies surrounding Confederate statues and flags, Columbus Day, Thanksgiving, *Gone with the Wind*, and Disney's *The Song of the South*.

Rather than taking the Bible as a neutral source of objective historical information, historical-critical scholars interrogate it—not viciously, but responsibly—to see where history might be found. This is done by (1) carefully reading the often very complicated original Hebrew of the Bible to look for evidence of when these stories were written and, more important, *why* they were written, and (2) bringing alongside the Bible evidence from outside of the Bible, namely, archaeological artifacts and stories written by other ancient people groups that have some relevance to and overlap with the biblical stories. In other words, historical-critical scholars seek to read the Bible carefully and understand the Bible's ancient context.

On both of these points, a lot has been discovered over the past two to three hundred years, which keeps scholars and doctoral students quite busy. Some historical evidence we have meshes nicely with parts of the Bible, which is to say that the Bible does have historical value.

Quite often, however—more often than not, it seems—the evidence paints a different picture of the past than what the Bible presents. The ultimate goal is to sift through the evidence within and outside of the Bible in order to paint a picture of Israel's origins that is truer to what actually happened. That portrait is typically called a "historical reconstruction."

I do not, however, mean to paint a rosy picture of historical criticism. Biases and blind spots are as much a part of this field as any other. And the very fact that historical-critical scholars often debate each other with veins popping and fists clenched (I've been to the meetings) suggests that not every idea that comes from the halls of academia is as solid as predicting the orbit of a comet; the study of history is a soft science with a dash of art. But few will deny that historical-critical scholarship has made tremendous advances in our understanding of the historical dimension of the Bible.

I would also like to make clear that the Bible is more than damaged historical goods, and I am not at all suggesting that the significance of the Bible can be reduced to questions of historical accuracy. The Bible has spiritual value that has always transcended such things. In fact, the ancient compilers of the Bible clearly understood that or they would not have been so intent on including contradictory accounts of the history of Israel and of Jesus.[1] But, if anyone reading the Bible today is at all curious about what happened two to three thousand years ago in the Levant (the common academic term for the land of the Bible), historical criticism is your unavoidable conversation partner. And with respect to Israelite origins, the historical evidence has on the whole not been particularly friendly for biblical literalism.

Okay, back to Abraham and my Maytag moment. According to a literal reading of Genesis, around 2000 BCE Abraham was called by God out of Haran (about two hundred miles north of Israel in modern-day Syria) to be the father of the nation of Israel, promising him both the land of Canaan as a possession and descendants as numerous as the stars in the sky and the sand on the shore. After many years, Abraham and his heretofore barren wife, Sarah, now in their nineties, finally had a son, Isaac, by direct divine intervention. Isaac in turn begat Abraham's grandchildren, the fraternal twins Jacob and Esau. Jacob had twelve sons (and one daughter), whose descendants would eventually form the twelve tribes of Israel after the exodus from Egypt under Moses. They then invaded Canaan and seized it for their own, and after a couple of hundred years the tribes combined to form the nation of Israel. And all of this was guided by God's hand.

From a historical-critical point of view, however, Israel's origins are vastly more complicated, which is what the study of history tends to do—to venture beneath the surface and reveal complexities. Rather than the Israelites descending in an orderly manner from one couple, the historical evidence suggests another scenario: The Israelites were not one people but a melting pot of various groups from various regions, including the land of Canaan itself. Over time, these people came to have a unified sense of self while evolving culturally, linguistically, politically, and religiously on their way to becoming the "Israel" we see in the Bible.

Bottom line: Biblical scholars do not treat Genesis as a book of history (even if they discern whiffs of history here and there). Rather, it is a collection of traditions that began orally (how far back is hard to tell) and were written down only much later, during the period of Israel's monarchy (which lasted from about 1000 to 586 BCE) and then in the wake of their exile to Babylon (after 586 BCE), which officially brought an end to the kingdom of Israel.

In fact, Genesis gives enough clues for scholars to think that the author probably lived during the period of the monarchy. He seems to have adapted the ancient traditions of his people for a new purpose: to tee up the story of Israel's monarchy from the time of David onward.[2] In other words, ancient Israelites shaped their ancient premonarchic traditions to reflect the interests of the monarchic period and beyond. This is somewhat analogous to Arthur Miller's *The Crucible*.[3] Sure, on the surface it may have been about the long-gone, seventeenth-century Salem witch trials, but the play was no dive into history for the sake of it. The deeper purpose was Miller's courageous commentary on McCarthyism of the 1950s. Both Miller and the writer of Genesis were more storytellers for the present than historians of the past.

A Little Breathing Room

That's a lot to take in, of course. It was a bit of a shock to my system as well—recall my Maytag moment. I had never even heard about Abraham's potential non-personhood before, and it certainly was never on the table as a possible historical option for people who take the Bible "seriously." Rather, "God's word is never wrong about history" is a literalist boundary that is not to be crossed. But in graduate school, far from the vaunted domain of biblical literalism, the idea seemed to be not in the slightest bit controversial.

For me, graduate school was largely a process of catching up with a broader conversation about the Bible and watching the literalist boundary expand, strain, and then give way altogether. This process would lead to some significant adjustments about the Bible and how I understood God. In short order I would wrestle with the main insights of historical criticism, all of which were well outside of my familiar boundaries, but all of which would come to make more and more sense to me, such as:

- *Not just Genesis, but any biblical books that deal with history are not so much accounts of "what happened" back in the day, but religious and political lessons to be learned for the writer's audience.*

- *Many biblical books were written by anonymous authors living generations and even centuries after the events they describe.*

- *The Bible is not truly a "book" but an anthology of ancient texts written over about a one-thousand-year span of time and that contain diverse and contradictory points of view.*

- *The Hebrew Bible as we know it did not exist until centuries after the sixth-century BCE Babylonian exile when it was brought together by anonymous scribes.*

- *The biblical writings are not fully unique but reflect cultural assumptions of antiquity and thus contain myth, legend, and folklore.*

Scholars continue to debate the particulars, but the broad outlines of these insights are not seriously challenged in academia—even if they are troublesome for biblical literalism.

I certainly found myself outside of the familiar evangelical terrain. But despite the discomfort, or perhaps because of it, I found myself drawn to what I was learning. It was a breath of fresh air—sometimes a cold bracing blast, but fresh nonetheless. Things were changing for me and I *liked* it, not because I was a theological Evel Knievel bent on driving my life into a canyon, but because what I was studying felt true and honest—and doesn't God value truth and honesty? I quickly intuited why questioning the literal truth of the Bible was so normal outside of my conservative circles: it was compelling. Not sexy, or trendy, or feeding our need for novelty, or rebellious against God, but compelling. It tied together loose ends, some of which I never knew existed, and presented a coherent picture of some uncooperative historical details.

By contrast, my older ways of thinking about the Bible didn't explain very much. Instead, in order to survive, those older ways had to be defended tooth and nail despite the evidence. Is that what God wants from us? Is that what faith is really supposed to be about—hanging on for dear life despite what you see? I hope not. In graduate school I found an understanding of the Bible that didn't require me to keep making excuses for it to myself or others. The sacred text was becoming for me less a rule book or owner's manual, and more an object of curiosity and exploration—an invitation rather than a burden.

Historical criticism isn't for everyone, and it need not be. I have known many wonderful Christians and Jews who don't care in the slightest about such things. But for those for whom the connection between history and faith is important, questions will arise for whatever reason—be it graduate school, bumping into a random article on the internet, or a History Channel documentary. It's hard to turn a blind eye to the challenges of history and how they play a role in questioning religious assumptions.

As for me, my doctoral work was the true beginning of my journey to find some way for my world of faith and my world of scholarship to coexist authentically. I was in the early stages of a path that would lead to a number of adjustments to how I thought about God, faith, and life itself.

A Better Bible and a Better God

It's possible that by now the point of all of this might have gotten lost in the details, though I've tried my best to keep the details to a bare minimum. But here is the point.

My view of the Bible changed because I committed myself to reading it and not turning a blind eye to what I was seeing. I happened to have done that in a highly structured setting, but you don't need to enter a doctoral program to start wrestling with the Bible. You don't need to know Greek or Hebrew, or the ins and outs of archaeology, or very much at all about the ancient religions and cultures that no doubt influenced, and even shaped, the biblical writers. One only needs to read the Bible in one's native language and with a curious and open mind.

I mention this because, I presume, a good number of you have already done that and found plenty of things in the Bible that have deeply challenged you. You may have collided with the violence that God commits or commands, the endless laws or tales of corrupt kings that seem out of sync with our daily lives, the contradictions, the wide gulf between ancient ways and modern science, or, as we've been looking at, its historical problems. Whatever the specifics, the simple act of reading the Bible carefully tends to undermine the notion that the Bible is God's flawless, set-in-stone, authoritative word downloaded to us.

I admit that there is something attractive about the Bible as a perfect set of instructions, but studying the Bible led me to conclude that this is not the Bible we have. To hold on to the Bible as I might want it to be despite the evidence to the contrary would be like laboring in a codependent relationship—tiptoeing around obvious problems just to keep the relationship alive when we know deep down it's toxic. With respect to the Bible, I believe the solution is not to end the relationship, but—as Jews and Christians have been doing for millennia—to learn how to rebuild it on a foundation of honesty that can strengthen the relationship and bring to it true adult intimacy. I am not interested in keeping my relationship with God on life support, but in seeing it thrive and grow. To do that, adjustments are in order.

Leaving behind the counseling metaphor, facing the Bible and accepting it for what it is—a messy, complex, dense mine of wisdom—has given me a more flexible view of the Bible, one where I do not expect it to be a step-by-step field guide to faith. And here is our payoff of all this, and which sets up the rest of this book:

> *The more flexible we are when it comes to reading the Bible,*
> *the more prepared we will be to adjust to the curveballs of*
> *life. The more inflexible we are, the less prepared we will be*
> *to make those adjustments precisely at the time when they*
> *will be needed to keep our faith alive and thriving.*

I do not believe that the Bible is a stand-in for God; God is not far off attending to other affairs, leaving us a book of instructions so we can make do. Rather, the Bible—in all its weird cultural foreignness—is a means of deepening our communion with a God who is ever-active and ever-present with us here and now. The Bible ties us to centuries of tradition by giving us language to express the joys and struggles we encounter. It models for us wisdom for seeing that this complex, flawed, beautiful sacred text points us, in its abruptly ancient and strangely foreign ways, toward God rather than having us think that God is pinned down by it, or that we are in good standing with God only when we take every sentence as literal and unimpeachable truth.

But there is something more to it. We seek a better way of reading the Bible not for its own sake, but to cultivate a better vision of what God is like—a God who is by definition out ahead of us, our tradition, and even the sacred text itself. And that sums up this chapter well. As I see it, the Bible is the sacred text of Christianity, but the God to which it points us is nevertheless far out ahead of it. God is not lurking behind bidding us to retreat back into the pages of a rule book. God is out ahead, drawing us forward—and the Bible, which is a *living* tradition, can help us see that.

I believe God expects us to be ready to adjust our beliefs when the curveballs come, to become better hitters, to play the game with greater skill and knowledge. And with that renewed vision of God, we might be able to see the broader role that sacred texts can play in our world. They offer their readers narratives for understanding their place in the world and even the cosmos—sacred texts help us work out the meaning of it all. Our job as readers of these texts and worshipers of God is to transpose those narratives from the ancient world into our own. As Cardinal Joseph Ratzinger (Pope Benedict XVI) puts it (italics added):[4]

[In Scripture] older texts are reappropriated, reinterpreted, and read with new eyes in new contexts. *They become Scripture by being read anew*, evolving in continuity with their original sense, tacitly corrected and given added depth and breadth of meaning. This is a process in which the word gradually unfolds its inner potentialities, already somehow present like seeds, but needing the challenge of new situations, new experiences and new sufferings, in order to open up.

By contrast, the Bible can be very limiting if we parse these ancient texts for exact alignment with what we know of history and science today. But they can be life-giving if we allow them to point us beyond the texts and bring them into conversation with the grand story of the cosmos and humanity as we experience it today. When read that way, sacred texts can shape our understanding of each other as human beings inhabiting a creation where all is connected.

We'll talk more about creation, connection, and God being out ahead of us in the chapters to follow, but for now let me simply say that we need a Bible that will help us embrace the hugeness of God's mystery, not keep us from it. Seeing the wisdom and beauty of a Bible like that occurred to me only because I was forced to wrestle with it. And as it turns out, wrestling with God and scripture is very old and completely normal. It's actually God-activated.

Chapter 3

Welcome to a New Normal

S OME YEARS AGO—thirty years after my blown elbow and twenty after graduate school—I found myself in a taxi in San Francisco on my way to a church to get paid money to talk about God. The midday traffic was heavy and the lights conspired to turn red whenever we got close to an intersection, so it took a while and my mind began to wander.

The fall day was bright and crisp, and the streets were abuzz with the eager lunchtime crowd evacuating their office buildings, mothers pushing strollers, couples window shopping, and enough homeless people to remind me that not everyone gets to be driven in a taxi and paid by a church to talk about God.

For whatever reason, that day I was struck by how many people were out and about. I tried guesstimating just those in my line of sight, but that quickly proved unworkable. It's hard to guesstimate a teeming swarm.

So there I was in the taxi, flown in to talk about God, surrounded by the proverbial mass of humanity, and I began to wonder how many of these people were like me. How many think about God as I do? How many think about God at all? How many of them would even have the slightest interest or patience to listen to the very important things I am being paid to say? And . . . what does God think of them for being that way?

So many people.

How many intersections does San Francisco have where this same moment is being played out? And how many cities and intersections are there across the country—and the world? And for how many generations have there been busy streets like this and for how many more generations will this be so? So many people, and I'm just one of them—with the audacity to judge them according to my standard.

My default image of God had me drawing thick lines between people like me and people not like me. Even if I didn't openly talk that way, my default image had old and deep roots that surfaced when I wasn't paying attention. Those not like me were less-than, beyond God's Presence, and (I suppose) damned to hell for eternity, or at least in some other very deep trouble, unless they became like me. I never liked the hell part of that calculus, to be honest, but that afternoon the entire formula just didn't sit right with me.

I mean, in theory the math works: you're either on the right side of the divine ledger book or not, and those who aren't, need what I and others like me have. There are even Bible verses to support the idea that line-drawing is something God is in full support of: "if you confess with your lips that Jesus is Lord and believe in your heart that God raised him from the dead, you will be saved" (Rom 10:9), which seems to imply the opposite if one does not confess. Or "There is salvation in no one else [Jesus], for there is no other name under heaven given among mortals by which we must be saved" (Acts 4:12). But those words were written long ago and far away. For me on that fall day, my thoughts of a God who draws familiar lines felt . . . inadequate . . . an affront to common sense.

The traffic conspired to hold me captive to an increasingly anxious train of thought: *maybe when it comes to God I don't have the slightest idea what I'm talking about.* Surrounded by an ocean of people with histories, hopes, dreams, pains, sorrows, shadows, joys, fears—in other words, people just like me—I was struck by a moment of searing existential clarity: Who am I to pass judgment on the population of San Francisco, even if my Christian tradition says it's my job to do so? Maybe I shouldn't presume what God is thinking about them. Maybe I should just shut up for a few years and think it all through. Or better, maybe I should just do golf course maintenance for the rest of my life.

With each stoplight I felt less and less qualified to talk to anyone about anything having to do with God, let alone in exchange for cash. What God was up to seemed less familiar to me than it had a few short minutes earlier. What I did know that moment, however, was that whatever version of God I was peddling was fragile enough to be thrown off balance by a few moments of unguarded reflection on a busy street in the solitude of stop-and-go traffic. I only hoped I could make it through the weekend without falling apart—and that the check would clear.

During that taxi ride I felt shame—or to put that in Christianese, I felt "convicted by the Holy Spirit"—about how easily I had let that default image linger deep down all these years. And the thing is, I really felt like God was trying to tell me something. This wasn't me going rogue, letting my rebellious mind forage through forbidden forests of bad theology just because I felt like it. I actually *didn't feel like it*. My anxiety was spiking. I had been just fine riding along thinking highly of myself on my way to dispensing wisdom to paying customers, and now, BAM!, my grip was slipping.

But I believe—without question—that God's Presence was with me in that taxi, pulling the cozy covers off me, pushing me out of my slumber, and throwing me out into a cold, dark 5 a.m. wake-up shower. I knew deep down this jolt was just what I needed, but I was also very uneasy about where all this would go. How *much* would my understanding of God change? Is this the slippery slope I was always warned about? And what would people think of me if they ever found out? I was staring down into a dark hole. I knew I had to jump down, but with no guarantees of how deep the drop or what I would find once I hit bottom.

I was living another curveball moment, another blown elbow. I found myself wrestling with God, or at least with my understanding of God, which would lead me to adjust my view of God from a deity who draws thick lines to one who, in whatever mysterious way, cares for all of us more deeply than I can fathom and who has all of creation in a relentless, loving embrace. That taxi ride, where my view of God was threatened, was actually a God moment. God upsetting my view of God—isn't that something?

And yet, that's the way it works. It always has.

Adjusting Our God-Talk Goes Way Back

Here's a fun fact from the Bible that, even though I teach the Bible for a living, I never really got until I was ready to see it.

In the book of Genesis, Jacob, the grandson of Abraham, is journeying home after a long hiatus in the far-off northern land of Haran. He knows he will soon be reunited with his elder brother, Esau, whom he sorely cheated out of his birthright and blessing decades earlier, and is now rightly concerned that he might get what is coming to him. Left alone with these troublesome thoughts, Jacob suddenly finds himself wrestling all night with "a man," though it seems clear as the story unfolds that this is no man but God (who sometimes shows up in the Bible looking very humanlike).

It was apparently quite a struggle, for, to get free, the divine combatant had to pull a trick move that put Jacob's hip out of joint, leaving him with a limp, yet even then Jacob would not release his grip. To end the contest, Jacob insisted the visitor first bless him, who responded by changing Jacob's name: "You shall no longer be called Jacob, but Israel, for you have striven with God and with humans, and have prevailed" (Gen 32:28). The divine being departed, and Jacob—now Israel—named the place Peniel ("face of God") saying, "I have seen God face to face, and yet my life is preserved" (Gen 32:30).

To sum up, God visits Jacob, and the next minute they are rolling around on the ground giving each other headlocks—and God started it.

Baked into the name "Israel" is this very idea of a divinely initiated wrestling match. And this name, "you have striven with God," the ancient biblical storyteller claimed, was not one that the people of Israel chose for themselves but one God bestowed upon them . . . *as a blessing.*

So, here is my late-blooming insight: perhaps wrestling with God is God-initiated and a blessing. Why is it a blessing? Because we never come out of that wrestling match as we entered. Wrestling with God may leave us limping, but it transforms our understanding of who God is. We see God better after the struggle.

Historically speaking, what the Hebrew word "Israel" means and how there came to be a people called by that name are complicated matters with several moving parts and no definitive answer. But that isn't our concern here. The ancient Israelites, when they wrote down their stories (again, during the monarchy and later), took "Israel" and ran with it. They saw in their obscure name a phrase that sounded like the combination of two Hebrew words: *yisra* ("he has striven") and *el* (God). Whatever the name's obscure historical origins, the ancient Israelites chose to understand it as a description of the type of relationship they had with their God—a relationship marked by God-initiated struggling.

At its core, the Israelite national self-concept was of a people who wrestled with God, and who intended to hold on to God and keep God in the struggle for as long as it took to get God to respond.

The ancient Israelites didn't seem to have the slightest intention of hiding their wrestling with God, and not simply here in this story of a name change: struggling with God marks the biblical story of Israel from beginning to end. Sometimes their struggles were their own darn fault for refusing to follow God's ways—like the story of Adam and Eve getting kicked out of the Garden of Eden. Other times, however, the struggle was due to no fault of their own. They were simply puzzled, panicked, or perturbed about God acting out of character with no explanation. We see this in the book of Psalms, where, for example, a psalmist is lamenting why God is so oblivious to the unjust suffering of the righteous while God lets the wicked go unpunished.

One story from the Bible that illustrates this type of unexpected wrestling with God is the story of the prophet Jonah—the guy swallowed by a large fish, forever a staple of children's Bible lessons, though that part is not the story's centerpiece.

God commanded Jonah to go to the Assyrian capital of Nineveh (in modern-day Iraq) and tell the Assyrians to repent. That might not strike us as a compelling storyline, but no Israelite with any cultural memory would expect something like this from their God. The Assyrians of Israel's memory were something like ISIS, raining terror on lesser nations, treating those who resisted ruthlessly. One object of Assyria's lust for world domination was the land of Israel—specifically the northern part of the once united nation founded around 1000 BCE,[1] but which split into northern and southern factions around 930 BCE, after the death of King Solomon, David's son. This northern nation was eventually conquered by the Assyrians in 722 BCE, never to rise again.

To sum up, the Israelites didn't like the Assyrians, and for good reason. In fact, another biblical prophet, Nahum, didn't like them either.

He wrote about how Assyria's violent end at the hands of the Babylonians (which happened in 612 BCE) was actually God's payback for their hostility. They were given no chance to repent, and the whole world rejoiced at Nineveh's destruction.

So, when God tells Jonah to give the Assyrians a chance to repent and thus possibly be forgiven by the God of the very people they mercilessly harassed, that's a big deal—and an unexpected move on God's part. One can hardly blame Jonah for refusing God's direct command and running away (which is what led to his being swallowed by a big fish and vomited up again). Jonah is panic-stricken that the Assyrians might actually take God up on the offer and repent rather than be wiped off the face of the earth as they deserved. In the story, the Assyrians do indeed repent, which leads to some soul searching on Jonah's part, not to mention a bit of whining at the end of the book.

Anyway, the story of Jonah is not a lesson in history. In fact, the author seems to be quite intent on his readers grasping that fact. Not only does a large fish swallow a human being who emerges alive after three days of being underwater in the belly of the fish, but historically speaking the mighty Assyrians never repented of anything because a Hebrew prophet told them to. They were, however, conquered by the Babylonians, in keeping with Nahum's words.

Rather, the story of Jonah is an object lesson—a story about Israel *adjusting its understanding of God*: God now has compassion on a nation that was responsible for relocating, assimilating, and making disappear roughly 80 percent of the Chosen People (not to mention harassing the remaining southern nation for a few decades thereafter). Our author poses not a God of uncompromising harsh judgment; rather, in his fictional story, he is posing a question: What if God is not our private deity who aims to wipe out our enemies? What if our god Yahweh has room in His heart for everyone, even the people we hate most?

This adjustment didn't come out of the blue. It grew out of an experience—a curveball that Israel had to adjust to, namely, the sixth-century BCE Babylonian exile.

Most scholars suggest that the author of Jonah lived in the wake of this national tragedy. Living side by side with the enemy, our author came to see the Babylonians as people, rather than simply as objects of God's wrath. As a nation, sure, the Babylonian war machine was "evil," but on the ground, in the day to day, as the captives got to know their Babylonian neighbors, they began to see them as people just like them—people who were Babylonians by birth, not choice, and were simply trying to farm, tend their livestock, raise their families, and generally not die. *Are these Babylonians really any different from us? Maybe—dare we hope?—God cares about them just as God cares about us.* That is the adjustment that the author of Jonah had to make, and he used the long-gone Assyrian enemies to make his rhetorical point.

I'm not sure how this story was received by the original audience, but I'd have to guess that not everyone simply would have gone along with such an about-face to their understanding of God. Yahweh was Israel's warrior-God, who had a long history of defeating Israel's enemies in Egypt and Canaan. How could this God now, without explanation, give aid and comfort to a nation that terrorized God's Chosen People? It's not hard to imagine our author getting some serious pushback from his more literalist country folk. Asking a community to adjust its traditions about God never goes unchallenged.

Maybe the whole point of my being stuck in stop-and-go traffic was to experience a kind of exile in San Francisco, of getting to see other people as just like me and to adjust my long-held view of God as a tribal deity who cares only for God's own.

It took me a while to see this, though. Twenty years before my taxi ride, while in my doctoral program, I had already been faced with an adjustment similar to Jonah's—yes, my default view of God was still lurking twenty years later in a San Francisco taxi. Old habits die slowly. My classmates and professors came from many walks of life, various countries, and numerous religious backgrounds, few of which remotely resembled my own. And as I lived and studied side by side with them for five years, my aforementioned default view of God began to seem ridiculous.

Were they really God's enemies in need of a good dose of white suburban evangelicalism? Would that even work? Is their adopting my ways any more likely than my adopting their Judaism, Islam, or atheism? They were born under certain circumstances and had life experiences that shaped them into what they were, and their ways were as strange to me as my ways were to them. Am I on the right side of the universe simply because I was born where I was, to German immigrants who lived near a church where I could accept Jesus as my savior? Plus, my graduate school comrades were often much nicer and generally less neurotic and combative than many Christians I had known. Were they really bound for hell when they died?

Those years were my first real experience of living alongside people way outside my familiar boundaries. It was the first time my mind was cracked opened to consider—in real time, not at a safe distance—that my view of what God was up to in the universe might be sorely inadequate and in need of adjustment to account for what my experience was forcing me to face. I was having a Jonah-like theological shift, one my subconscious had kept buried for years lest my community start giving me the stink eye.

No Thanks, We're Good

According to the main biblical storyline, Israel's God was mightier than any of the other gods of the other nations, and the Israelites were

God's own Chosen People. These two beliefs—Yahweh's invincibility and Israel's chosenness—led the Israelites to believe that no harm would come to their nation. Specifically, since God's home of sorts was the temple in Jerusalem, one might expect the almighty and faithful God to be fiercely protective of it. And with God at their side, the Israelites would produce a line of kings descended from King David that would last "forever"[2] and thus shine as a beacon for the world to see. These were the promises of God, at least as the ancient Israelites understood them.

But all this came to an end in 586 BCE, when, after a decade of pressure, King Nebuchadnezzar and the mighty Babylonians sacked Jerusalem, razed the sacred temple to the ground, killed off the Davidic line, and deported the Jerusalem elite to a distant and foreign land. This was Israel's blown elbow moment: How can our God let this happen to us?

Fair question. In those days, gods were national deities and tribal war leaders. The gods of defeated nations were deemed inferior, since they clearly couldn't protect their people. Yahweh was Israel's warrior-God, but rather than suggesting Yahweh was defeated by the Babylonians, the standard biblical response to this horrific defeat was to present it as all Yahweh's idea to begin with—it was punishment for Israel's rank unfaithfulness. Their return to their homeland in 539 BCE was also seen as a God moment—God delivered the captives by God's unfailing (even if slow) mercy. The whole thing, exile and return, was an act of God's sovereign power, not evidence of God's weakness. Faith crisis resolved.

Others, however, were not particularly moved by this main storyline and instead made a *major* adjustment to their view of God, but one that never seems to get the airtime it deserves, at least with Christians. When the moment came to bask in God's favor and return home from exile, not all the captives were elbowing their way to the front of the line to get out of Babylon. Some took their sweet time (several decades). Others decided to stay behind and make a permanent home in a foreign land.

Think about that. For centuries, Israel's default view of God was one where possession of the Promised Land, the sacred operations of the temple, and the stable monarchy were considered sure signs of God's Presence among them. Surely, for some to decide to stay behind when the opportunity arose to get that all back again took a rather massive adjustment of what it meant to be God's people living in God's will. So often in the Bible, being outside of the land of Israel was seen as being apart from God's Presence, even as a form of death. And yet when the time came, many decided they didn't want to go back to the old country. Death was transformed to life: "We can be Israel here, in a foreign land. For us this is the place to carve out a new existence as children of father Abraham."

Again, it's hard to imagine this scenario playing out without some conflict. Perhaps those who returned home thought that those who stayed behind were weak-kneed slackers happy to assimilate with the pagan Babylonians. Sure, that may have happened. I'd be willing to bet it did, but the part of the story we do know about is different. In time, Babylon would become the major religious center for Jews, which would last a thousand years—twice as long as the nation of Israel itself existed. The sacred book of Judaism, the Babylonian Talmud, which is studied to this day, was crafted in Babylon—a Palestinian Talmud would also be compiled in the old homeland, but it never had the authority of the Babylonian version. Had these Jews not remained behind, *Judaism as we know it would not exist.*

Those who stayed were people of faith, desiring to live as God's people. The experience of these exiles in the new world led them to adjust their understanding of what it meant to be faithful to the God of old. Rather than weeping by the rivers of Babylon over their lost homeland (Psalm 137), God was now believed to support something that a scant fifty years before would have been unthinkable. Those Judahites who returned (later called Judeans) get all the attention in the Bible, but that's because they are the ones who wrote the stories.

Adjustments Just Kept Going

Let's not get lost in the details. I am simply pointing out that making adjustments in understanding God is part of the biblical tradition. And as the centuries passed, Jews would make many other adjustments to their views of God in order to adapt to the realities of their world.

Of the many we could touch on, one quick and crucial example will make the point: the influence of Greek culture. After 250 years of foreign domination—first by the Babylonians and then the Persians—a twenty-three-year-old Greek stud named Alexander the Great took over most of the known world, including the land of Judea in 332 BCE. This is a huge time period in Jewish history. Adjusting some of its beliefs to Greek culture would prove foundational not only for the future of Judaism but for Christianity as well.

Greek culture was nothing like Hebrew culture. The Greeks had philosophy, architecture, and science; they talked about the nature of meaning, the existence of atoms, and the curvature of the earth. Quite an ambitious and accomplished group of people, I'd say. The Israelites, by contrast, were a conquered people, ex-slaves. They had no science or philosophy, just a book of ancient tribal stories and a massive compendium of legal codes—along with the words of the prophets chiding them for not keeping them. Jewish culture seemed quaint by comparison, somewhat out of place in the polished world of Greek sophistication—like someone showing up at a posh, catered house party in cut-off jeans and a tank top.

The ins and outs of the relationship between the ancient Greeks and the Jews living in Judea is tricky, and historians are right to remind us of it. But Greek culture most definitely had a significant impact on how Jews thought about what it meant to be connected to their ancient faith—and that led to some rather remarkable adjustments.

One place where we can see Greek influence might be surprising, but that's only because we—especially Christians—are so used to it. Christians effortlessly talk of God as all-powerful, all-knowing, and being in all places at once—omnipotent, omniscient, and omnipresent—like nothing could be more obvious. But those ways of talking about God were at best minimally promoted in the Hebrew Bible, if at all, with plenty of examples to the contrary. Rather, these three "omnis" came to Christianity through Greek influence on ancient Judaism.

The Hebrew Bible doesn't really talk about God using the three omnis,[3] but Greek philosophers did when talking about the ultimate being in the universe, and their language was eventually adopted by Jews when speaking of their God. In fact, for one very well-known Jewish thinker of the time, Philo of Alexandria (ca. 20 BCE to 50 CE), Moses was no mere lawgiver. He was upgraded to the status of Israel's philosopher, and Torah became Israel's book of philosophy on par with Greek literature. And if Philo is any indication, it seems pretty clear, too, that at least some Jews saw these adjustments as God-led improvements on the old ways of thinking.

Adjustments to Greek culture weren't just talked about in bars, restaurants, and bowling alleys. They went right to the heart of things: adjustments were officially embedded in Israel's sacred scripture—namely, in the Greek translations of their own Hebrew scriptures, which became necessary as Greek became the dominant language of Judaism.

For example, in the Hebrew version of the story of Noah and the flood in Genesis, we read that God sent the flood because he was "sorry" he had created humans and was grieved "to his heart" (Gen 6:6) about it because these humans did nothing but sin all the time. I imagine some of you might be put off at the thought of the almighty and all-knowing Creator expressing frail human emotions like regret and grief. That's only because we're the heirs to two thousand years of Greek and Western influence on an ancient Middle Eastern religion. The Jewish translators of this story into Greek also seemed to have been put off by this, and so they translated the Hebrew to make God look more godlike and less like an upset parent taken by surprise: rather than God being *sorry* and *grieved*, the translators said God *thought deeply* and *pondered* the situation. Yahweh has become a more calm, cool, collected, and rational deity, one worthy of being taken seriously by sophisticated Greeks.

There are volumes more to say about this period of Jewish history, and we could go through much more of it, but (1) you would probably hate me for it, and (2) it would all lead to the same punch line:

Judaism has a history of adjusting the faith of old to meet the challenges of the new, which, as we've seen, began already in the pages of the Hebrew scriptures themselves.

When the twists and turns of history came their way, Jews did not respond simply by holding on tooth and nail to old ways of thinking, but by adjusting the faith of old—no doubt with great soul-searching and debate—in order for the ancient faith to make sense for them there and then, and thus to ensure its continued vitality.[4]

These adjustments were not made with as little thought as changing your T-shirt. It takes a lot of wrestling and discomfort for some members of any religious group to say that their views of the group need to adapt to the present circumstances, and those who suggest such a thing are more often hailed as foe rather than friend. And yet, the faith of the biblical writers and of Jews after the exile was flexible enough to adjust when the situation called for it. Many of those adjustments were ultimately adopted as part of Jewish tradition, and as such were seen as acts of faith, not a rejection of it.

And with that we get to take our first commercial break in this book: *historically speaking, it sure looks like adjusting one's understanding of God is pretty normal.*

Because it is.

My own curveballs (blown elbows, a taxi ride, and graduate school) were similar to what we've been looking at. The God whom I understood was inadequate for addressing the world I lived in. I was honest with myself about this uncomfortable feeling, and I learned through it that the Bible itself, not to mention the history of my faith tradition, modeled for me that very process of adjusting our understanding of God to address the realities of our existence.

I understand the concerns some might have about this train of thought, but I am not suggesting that anything I happen to utter on a whim after some bad shrimp will wind up being a lasting and positive adjustment. It only means that when I have my blown elbow moments, and I find my understanding of God to be inadequate to address the needs of those moments, I am not wrong to listen to my instincts and think with curiosity and in all seriousness, "Maybe my view of God is askew and needs to grow."

In working through the matter this way, I am not on shifting sand. In fact, without some rather significant adjustments, Christianity as we know it wouldn't even exist.

Chapter 4

Adjusting for Jesus

A S WE JUST SAW, for Jews living after the exile, the curveball they had to adjust to was the shock of the exile itself and then centuries of cultural influence from the dominant nations that ruled them. The world was changing and Judaism responded—in various ways, I might add.[1] For another group of Jews living during the Roman occupation of Judea (which began in 63 BCE), Jesus was the curveball. Their belief that Jesus was the Son of God led them to make other sorts of adjustments about God—rather unexpected and (for some) troubling ones—that touched the core of Jewish tradition.

It is no overstatement to say that the Christian faith, from the very beginning, has been in the business of making a series of significant adjustments to how its own Jewish tradition understood God. Early Christians did not reject their Jewish heritage, but adapted it to meet their moment. And the New Testament authors make no effort to tuck these adaptations away from prying eyes. They parade them front and center.

Watching how the New Testament authors adapted the faith of old for their moment in time has been a huge encouragement for me, even a lifeline. Adjusting our understanding of God when the circumstances

call for it is baked into the pages of Christianity's founding documents—
it is not simply acceptable but *vital* for faith to thrive and grow.

Not Your Father's Judaism

So how did the early followers of Jesus adjust their ancient Jewish
faith? One huge example concerns the Promised Land.

Throughout the Hebrew Bible, the Promised Land was seen as a
gift of God to the children of Abraham and a sign of God's favor toward them. This remained a core element of Israel's tradition long after
the exile ended, despite the fact, as we've seen, that many other Jews
bucked the system and remained in Babylon.

According to the Gospels, Jesus also bucked the system concerning
the land. In Jesus's day, at least some repatriated Jews were expecting God
to wrest control of the land from the Roman overloads by placing an
anointed king on the throne in Jerusalem as in the old days. This king
was called "Messiah" (Hebrew *mashiach*, "anointed one"), and "Christ"
(Greek *Christos*) is the Greek version of that word. So for Jesus to be called
"the Christ" is not some otherworldly divine designation but a statement
of belief that Jesus would be the king who would reverse Israel's sad,
centuries-long period of misfortune of being subjects in their own land.

We can appreciate the confusion created when Jesus showed absolutely no interest—zero, zip—in returning Israel to the days of old and
instead spoke of how his kingdom is "not of this world." *What are you
talking about, Jesus?! Not of this world?! Of course it is! Read your Bible!
Have you ever heard of what happened to our ancestors in the exile? And
just look at our recent history of foreign domination! Getting our land
back is the whole point!*

Not only was Jesus uninterested in Making Israel Great Again, but he suffered a fate one would not expect of a divinely appointed conquering king: he was crucified by the Romans as a common criminal, thus heaping shame on him, on anyone who would follow him, and especially on a God who seemed otherwise preoccupied or too weak to do anything about it.

Other would-be Jewish messiahs had already met the same fate in previous years, which simply underscores how Jesus's crucifixion would have been an obvious nonstarter in the Messiah department for Jew or Gentile alike. But that's not how the New Testament writers see it. In fact, paradoxically, they are adamant that crucifixion was actually crucial *for* Jesus's messianic agenda.

The curveball of the Messiah's crucifixion led to an adjustment about what God was up to—an adjustment that, on the face of it, made no sense. King Jesus inaugurated the "kingdom of heaven" *by* enduring the shame of the cross—and the God of Israel was willingly aligned with that act. A Messiah who was crucified and who had no interest in sacred geography had no place in Jewish thinking. But for those who believed, it was a curveball the likes of which Judaism had never experienced.

Speaking of crucifixion, another serious adjustment is that crucifixion was understood by the New Testament writers as a sacrifice. That is a very odd idea if you take a step back and look at it. True, in one strand of Judaism, the blood of martyrs worked like a sacrifice to God—atoning for the sins of the people.[2] But Jesus's crucifixion was seen as a sacrifice that *God made* on behalf of humanity. Sacrifices usually work the other way around—humans offer something of value to God, not God offering something of value for humans. The whole direction of what a sacrifice means is reversed. (And, incidentally, this is why it is wrong to think of Jesus's sacrifice as something Jesus did to calm God down and appease God's wrath. The crucifixion is a challenging and much-discussed topic in Christian theology, but fundamentally it is to be understood in the context of God's love, not anger.)

In both Jewish and Roman cultures, to say that the shameful crucifixion of Israel's Messiah is actually God's intention, a sacrifice God offers and Jesus willingly accepts on behalf of humanity, is not your lead if you are trying to promote a religion that will hope to convince anybody. And the fact is that the Jesus movement did not sweep across the land like a Taylor Swift single (not that I would know). The crucifixion of the Messiah required too big of an adjustment for many—as Paul put it, Christ crucified is "a stumbling-block to Jews and foolishness to Gentiles" (1 Cor 1:23).

One other crucial adjustment concerns the place non-Jews have in this Jewish Jesus movement. Parts of the Hebrew Bible look forward to a future time when the Gentile nations will stream to Jerusalem to worship the true God—Gentiles can be included in Judaism. But the apostle Paul, who wrote a major chunk of the New Testament, takes it a step further. In his letters, he argues with passion that Gentiles who believe in Jesus are now co-equal with Jews as children of Abraham. One implication is that Gentiles would not need to convert to Judaism to be true children of Abraham and followers of Jesus. In fact, the Jewish law was not in any way binding upon them. In one of his letters (Romans), Paul even strongly suggests that the law had already performed its main function, which was to get people to a place where faith in Christ rather than simply obedience to the law is the true mark of faith.

In other words, Gentiles *as Gentiles*, simply by virtue of their *faith in Jesus*, were equal partners with Jews in God's ultimate plan. By virtue of a crucified and resurrected Messiah, God reconciled Jews and Gentiles as equal in status. Christians may take that for granted today, but this represented a social and religious upheaval at the time.

Paul's report in the book of Galatians indicates that this idea greatly vexed other Jewish followers of Jesus, not the least of which were James, Jesus's brother, and the apostle Peter. They felt Paul had made too big of an adjustment to Jewish tradition. I can certainly see their point. Disagreements with Paul were bound to happen because the adjustment to the faith of Jewish tradition was so fundamental.

The adjustments that Paul and other New Testament writers made are what gave rise to Christianity as a distinct religion from Judaism. It didn't start out that way. Neither Paul nor Jesus had any intention of starting a new religion. Paul especially argued that Jesus Christ crucified and raised was, despite appearances, deep down God's way of moving the Abrahamic faith forward. But over time (by the second century CE) Christianity and Judaism would drift apart and become different religions, with Christianity largely populated by Gentiles.

So, here is my point. As distinct as Judaism and Christianity have become, they are united at least in this respect: *both have a history of making adjustments to their shared sacred scripture in light of unforeseen, even paradoxical, circumstances.* Jews adjusted their story to account for historical upheavals like the fall of the first temple at the hands of the Babylonians, Greek influence, and then the fall of the second temple at the hands of the Romans (in 70 CE). The writers of the New Testament (who were largely Jewish) adjusted the ancient story in light of their faith that Jesus was the crucified and raised Son of God.

In both cases, the tradition adapted in order to thrive. And I can't stress enough that the Christian faith is what it is because of the adjustments the New Testament writers made to their own ancient Jewish tradition. In other words, *Christianity is not a purely biblical religion but a living adaptive tradition of the ancient biblical witness.*

And So It Continues

Adjustments made by Christians to their understanding of God did not end with the New Testament writers. In fact, they took off. The

Jesus movement began as a Jewish faith, an inner dialogue within Jewish tradition and also in conflict with Rome, with the expectation that God's judgment to set everything right was just around the corner. But it soon shifted to a Gentile world with Gentile questions and answers—namely, philosophical ones. As the Christian faith spread in the generations to come throughout the Roman Empire and beyond, it essentially became a Gentile religion and was driven by Gentile concerns.

For example, the ancient church creeds (of the fourth and fifth centuries) talk about the God of ancient Jewish tradition in language steeped in Greek and Roman philosophy. The Nicene Creed (325 CE, amended in 381) speaks of Jesus as "God from God, Light from Light, true God from true God, begotten, not made, of one Being with the Father." John's Gospel (probably written in the 90s CE) comes somewhat close to this way of speaking,[3] but we generally don't find this language in the New Testament.

The Chalcedonian Creed (451 CE) is even more philosophical, describing Jesus as "truly God and truly man, of a reasonable [rational] soul and body; consubstantial [sharing the same essence] with the Father according to the Godhead, and consubstantial with us according to the Manhood." That's enough to wrap our heads around, but there's more. Jesus is "to be acknowledged in two natures, inconfusedly, unchangeably, indivisibly, inseparably; the distinction of natures being by no means taken away by the union, but rather the property of each nature being preserved, and concurring in one Person and one Subsistence, not parted or divided into two persons, but one and the same Son, and only begotten, God the Word, the Lord Jesus Christ."

This language hardly falls off our lips, and I sure hope there is no theology exam when we stand before God, unless we are given a few decades to bone up on Greco-Roman philosophy. And to be honest, I'd bet good money that Paul and even Jesus himself, as first-century Jews, wouldn't have known what to make of it all. But what else should we expect? The ancient creeds are not a repetition of the biblical language. They are adaptations of the tradition to reflect the questions that concerned people in their time and place in Christian history. Debates were flaring about Jesus, namely, what it meant for him to be the "Son of God." These ancient theologians used the philosophical language of their time and place to try to bring precision and clarity to those debates.

To what extent they succeeded in clarifying things is a matter of opinion (see above verbiage); my point is that the creeds, which have been so central to much of the history of the Christian faith, are not simply repeating what was in the Bible but building on it and thus *going beyond it.* The ancient faith was adjusted to speak to a new time and place in order to make the tradition meaningful *for the people in that time and place.* That's what happens when you try to keep a tradition going; to use the language of jazz, the tradition encourages improvisation, not conformity.

We could drop down at almost any point in church history (not to mention the history of Judaism) and talk about adjustments that were made in order to speak of God in ways that made sense at the time. This is why we have literally thousands of Christian churches and denominations that are separated by their distinct beliefs.[4]

Rather than thinking of all this diversity as a problem, it seems to me that it reflects the inevitable need of us humans to adjust to how we understand God by virtue of when and where we live and what issues we are facing.

It Really Matters

The point of all the wrestling and adjusting isn't just to change our understanding of God for the sake of it, but to find a better God because the circumstances demand it—meaning, to see that God is better than we thought. Paying attention to our curveballs and seeing them as invitations to take us beyond our familiar ideas of God is vital to a mature, meaningful, and hopeful life of faith.

For one thing, how we understand God has consequences for how we treat others. If we see God as drawing thick lines between groups of people, we will feel justified in doing so ourselves. If we believe God is vindictive, we are only a small step from justifying belligerence toward and even violence against "the other" in the name of God, an alarmingly recurring fact of Christian history that still thrives today in strands of Christian fundamentalism and Christian nationalism. Much more is at stake than just in-house fine-tuning of God to see which group of Christians comes up with the prize-winning version. What is at stake is a faith that can actually remain sustainable and meaningful because it listens to the challenges of the present as we follow the God who is always out ahead of us, ready to surprise us.

But of course, none of this is easy. A lot of heat is generated by wrestling through changes in what we believe, and not simply because our understanding of God is changing. The tensions arise because we also sense that some parts of our faith need to stay the same.

So here is another big point I want to make: *adjusting our understanding of God is never about throwing it all away and starting from scratch.* The wrestling happens precisely by bringing the old and new together somehow—bringing them into healthy, constructive conversation and exploring where all this is headed. This was the struggle of the ancient Jews under foreign occupation. It was also the struggle of the first followers of Jesus as they tried to bring together the old and new.

These conversations are a group effort, since the life of faith is more a symphony of voices than a twenty-minute head-banging drum solo. The fact that others are involved who might not see things the same way is exactly what makes the wrestling so painful at times. My Maytag moment and my anxiety in the taxi were largely about how my community of faith would react to my thoughts.

It would be nice simply to avoid it all and never make any adjustments, but does that even happen? Do our views of God really stand still our whole lives? We adjust because we exist, and our existence always finds a way of exposing the inadequacies of our understanding of God and how the universe works.

And I have to believe God understands that.

Like everyone who has ever gone before us, we can't help that we were born at a certain time and place, and under certain circumstances. Those times, places, and circumstances are precisely what *generate their own questions*, questions that are difficult to table.

Actually, they *should not* be tabled.

Maybe those questions that arise from our humanity are the very things we need to help us to see God in ways that point beyond our brief moment of time, to see God as leading us onward, past our limited imaginations. Maybe that's why adjustments tend to cluster around times of wrestling—the process is painful and our disjointed hips stay with us as a reminder of the need to keep an open mind and heart about how we understand God.

We do not enter into this struggle of our own accord. We do not will it to happen on a whim. Rather, "experiences happen." Like Jacob, we are confronted by God in the midst of our routines, and the very fact that adjusting our view of God is so grueling demonstrates the authenticity of the experience. Since when is unasked-for change painless? Whoever spread the rumor, anyway, that faith is smooth sailing?!—just an ascent to some ideas, to be held tightly, and that's that. What if a central feature of the life of faith is the very challenging of our ideas from one season to the next, to show us that all our thinking about God is to be held loosely to keep us from ever believing that our thoughts about God are permanently settled?

And what if the Bible—even the Bible—rather than being God's crisis prevention tool to settle our queries, is modeling for us the fact that those crises are normal and necessary, if also difficult and unsettling?

Faith is about more than being converted; it is a path to a deeper curiosity about and communion with the mystery of God. This, at least, is what I have found to be true, and it is my own experiences of blown elbows and other curveballs that have slowly nudged me to this realization over many years. And maybe this faith needs to be felt in our guts, in our whole bodies, not just our minds; in our right brains, not just our left; in our instincts, not just the earthquake-safe structures we build to keep our faith stable.

I have found that the prompts to adjusting my understanding of God are all around me—literally. The very heavens are shouting them, and the word they are shouting most clearly is "mystery."

Chapter 5

Blink of an Eye

I N SEPTEMBER OF 1977, as I was launching into my senior year of high school, some very smart humans launched not one but two spacecrafts the size of Mini Coopers in separate directions to explore our solar system and beyond. Along with all sorts of data-collecting instruments, Voyagers 1 and 2 were also outfitted with signs and sounds of our little planet engraved on a disk, in the off chance that other intelligent creatures will stumble on it in the next hundred billion trillion years or so and that they will have access to a CD player. Here's hoping.

Voyager 1 is still zipping along at 38,000 miles per hour, or about 10.5 miles per second. That's plenty fast for me. I'd love a two-second commute to work. It would change my life. And after more than forty years, this celestial go-kart has gone a whopping 14.1 billion miles, far outside of the sun's 10-billion-mile reach (known as the heliosphere). That's a lot of miles. To give a sense, it would take us about 447 years to count to 14.1 billion at one count per second. So, Voyager 1 has traveled very far indeed. Having said that, though, its pace is still pathetically slow on the cosmic scale. Light, the fastest thing in the universe, travels at 186,282 miles per second, and would cover that 14.1 billion miles in about twenty-one hours.

Yes, light is fast. But how fast, really? Fast enough that it eventually got me thinking differently about where I fit into God's universe—and what I mean by God at all.

The universe was a major league curveball for me. Not only its speed, but its size, age, and just general incomprehensibility. Looking back, I am horrified that I was never taught to allow what we have come to know about the universe to bleed into my understanding of God. Throughout my Christian education, which included seminary, we all seemed content to go on talking about God as "up there" and the heavens "above" in ways that are not so different from the perspective of the ancient biblical writers.

My big adjustment was in accepting that I would need to think of the cosmos differently from the way the biblical writers and most of the Christian tradition had thought of it. More to the point, I would also need to accept that my understanding of God would need to grow beyond what I had been taught my whole life.

The universe was telling me that adjustments were needed, and those words felt true and right. I knew I couldn't simply ignore what I knew about the cosmos. As a matter of integrity, I had to accept the challenge.

Way Faster Than My Fastball

Are you up for some audience participation? Good. Blink. Go ahead. Blink. I'm serious.

That blink took about 0.4 seconds. And while you blinked, light covered about seventy-five thousand miles. That's fifteen five-thousand-mile round-trip flights between New York and Los Angeles.

Humor me. Blink again and imagine sitting on a plane and covering fifteen round-trip cross-country flights during that blink. And if we hung on for a full second, we would make about thirty-seven such trips, covering 186,282 miles (or about seven and a half trips around the Earth's circumference).

I cannot process speed like this. I cannot even imagine thirty-seven discreet sequential events of any sort in one second. To bring it down to earth (I'm just trying to be helpful here), driving on the highway at sixty miles per hour, I would cover one-tenth of a mile in six seconds. In that same six seconds, light would cover more than 1.1 million miles—more than four times the distance to the moon.

Speaking of the moon, imagine being shot into space at the speed of light—you'd be dead, but hang with me. You would pass the moon in a little more than one second ("one one-thousand"), Mars in about twelve minutes (on average), likewise Jupiter in three-quarters of an hour, and Neptune in a whopping four hours—that's four uninterrupted hours of making thirty-seven cross-country round trips every second. Try to imagine that. I'm serious. Take ten seconds (during which light would travel 1,862,820 miles) and try. Maybe you can do it, but I can't. My brain just shuts down and starts humming *The Partridge Family* theme song ("Come on get happyyyyyyyyy").

On the cosmic scale, however, the distance to Neptune is a hair's width. Between Neptune and the nearest known star to Earth in our Milky Way galaxy (Proxima Centauri) lies a twenty-five-trillion-mile vacuum, which would take light about 4.25 years to cover. That's thirty-seven cross-country round trips every second . . . of every minute . . . of every day . . . for 1,550 days—five billion cross-country trips in all.

I simply can't imagine that number, and that's just the nearest star. Let's head on over to the nearest galaxy, Andromeda. How long would that take? A long time, that's how long. That baby is about 2.5 million light-years away—which comes to three thousand trillion cross-country trips. These numbers are incomprehensible, inhuman— which is more or less the point of my getting calculator happy for the past few paragraphs.

The universe is larger than I can imagine, and any explanation takes me far from my realm of experience—and I imagine yours, too. As the eighteenth-century Greek Orthodox theologian Nicodemus of the Holy Mountain put it, "The cosmos is an ocean that drowns every mind,"[1] which might be my first tattoo.

Speaking of drowning, here is another important angle on the bigness of it all. Our galaxy is between one hundred thousand and two hundred thousand light-years in diameter (read that again) and contains at the very least one hundred billion stars (read that again, too). If someone were to count to one hundred billion at one count per second, it would take (I assume you're sitting down) thirty-two hundred years. If an ageless person had started counting during the time of King David, they'd still have about two hundred more years to go. (Almost done! You've got this!) Some estimates are closer to four hundred billion stars, or nearly thirteen thousand years of counting.

And that's just our galaxy. Another several hundred billion galaxies (perhaps two or more trillion, let's see what the James Webb Space Telescope reveals) are waiting to have their stars counted, too. It is truly the case, as is often said, that there are as many stars in the universe as there are grains of sand on the seashore.[2]

You'd think with numbers like that the universe would be pretty jam packed, but no. Our trickster universe seems to be about 96 percent "empty space,"[3] which means it needs to be very large indeed to fit all those stars housed in galaxies tens or hundreds of thousands of light-years in diameter. And sure enough, it is. The entire universe, or at least that part of it we have detected, is about ninety-three billion light-years across. In miles that would be (since I took the time to figure it out) 547 sextillion miles (547 followed by twenty-one zeros). Whatever. It means nothing to me. Nothing at all, other than, "I give up."

Okay, we're done with numbers. To sum up, the cosmos is incomprehensibly large and largely empty, and inside this cosmos are incomprehensibly large galaxies that are incomprehensibly far apart from each other, and each one contains an incomprehensible number of stars. So here is my point: this information stuns me into silence when I try to "explain" God to myself. I mean, I spend a goodly amount of time each day wondering how I ran out of underwear so quickly. I'm just not sure what I can add to the God conversation. It's clearly out of my league.

And yet, questions continue to live rent-free in my head. How do I talk about God in light of all this? What do I even mean by "God" and where—or what—God "is"? What words do I have at my disposal to speak of God that actually give God due credit for all of this? I am at a loss for words. How can I not be?

All I know is that the God I am familiar with—the God spoken of in churches and books; the God high above looking down upon us from the heavenly throne; the God whose eye is on the sparrow; the God who prevents diseases and orchestrates whom we marry, what house we buy, where our kids go to college; the God who delays planes so we can catch the flight home—this God makes little sense to me against the backdrop of infinity. This God does not seem to be linked to the world in which we live and breathe, but to be more of a relic of days before modern cosmology. And since I live in this world and not another, I feel I need to work through how our current understanding of the cosmos affects my understanding of God, Jesus, the Bible, and a few other things.

Imagine That

The Bible is not much help in thinking through the implications of how an infinite universe might affect how we speak of God. Though the biblical God is not immune to making cameo appearances down on earth, that God's primary place of residence is most assuredly far off "up there" somewhere, a place so high "up" that we humans cannot attain it (though the builders of the Tower of Babel tried it, and the apostle Paul claims to have experienced it in a vision). Glimpses of God walking in the Garden of Eden, thundering atop Mount Sinai, showing the divine backside to Moses, and periodically residing in the temple are remarkable, which is to say, not the norm: God is fundamentally transcendent and other. God's Presence bursts through any and all earthly confinements, including Solomon's temple. As Solomon put it, "Even heaven and the highest heaven cannot contain you, much less this house that I have built!" (1 Kgs 8:27).

Even such a promising hint, however, will not help connect scripture to the world of modern cosmology. In biblical times (from what we can tell), the heavens of which Solomon spoke were not thought to be (for all intents and purposes) infinite but to be made up of successive layers, and the high god dwelt in the highest of them. (This is one reason why Israel's God is sometimes referred to by the superlative "most high" God.)

But such a striking claim does not account for a universe measured in billions upon billions of light-years. By calling their God "most high," the Israelites were simply claiming that Yahweh was the supreme deity, against whom none other in the relatively small divine realm could compare. If we choose to borrow that ancient idiom to speak of God in the context of modern cosmology, we should be clear what we are doing: adapting that language to something it was not designed to address. And that is fine by me, but let's just be upfront about what we are doing.

An ancient cosmos is still very much in view everywhere else in the Bible, including the New Testament, such as at the end of Matthew's Gospel. There, Jesus announces, "All authority in heaven and on earth has been given to me" (Matt 28:18). What Jesus means when he says "heaven" is not the cosmos you or I think of. Jesus's cosmos is small by comparison, much more aligned with "most high" than galaxies, quasars, and dark matter.

Squaring the biblical cosmos with our own is, to say the least, not easy. I do indeed wrestle with God's place in the heavens, despite the psalmist's lofty praise in Psalm 19: "The heavens are telling the glory of God; / and the firmament proclaims his handiwork" (v. 1). This is easy to say when your heavens are a solid dome high above (aka "the firmament") that separates the created world from the realm of the heavenly beings. The psalmist is praising God in terms of an ancient cosmos that no longer exists.

When I look up at the night sky, I see something else—an unsettling expanse that keeps expanding at speeds I cannot comprehend, a cosmos that continues still to evolve and that lays waste any thoughts I had about where or what God is. I'm more with seventeenth-century philosopher and mathematician Blaise Pascal:

> When I consider the short duration of my life, swallowed up in the eternity before and after, the little space which I fill, and even can see, engulfed in the infinite immensity of spaces of which I am ignorant, and which know me not, I am frightened, and am astonished at being here rather than there; for there is no reason why here rather than there, why now rather than then. Who has put me here? By whose order and direction have this place and time been allotted to me? . . . The eternal silence of the infinite spaces terrifies me.[4]

Pascal (1623–1662), a devout Catholic, lived in the wake of Copernicus, Galileo, and Kepler,[5] who succeeded in moving the earth from the center of a fairly contained "heavens" to simply the third among six known planets at the time and set against the backdrop of a very large cosmos. Rather than skipping along and happily quoting Psalm 19, Pascal is in full-on faith crisis mode brought on by the hugeness of it all. I get it. Not only was the earth decentered for Pascal, but the significance of his puny and temporary life was called into question. I can't imagine Pascal tolerating the thought of praying to God for dry weather for the church picnic or getting a good deal on a used horse.

Like Pascal, I also wonder about these things, though on a larger and more unnerving scale. Our "infinite spaces" are far more extensive than Pascal could have known. I stare out into a universe that began nearly 14 billion years ago, and I can't help but ask what it means to say "God" and how I or anything I do actually counts. Yes, "the eternal silence of the infinite spaces terrifies me," and especially so if in the back of one's mind are long-held images of a Zeus-like God who is "up there," taking up time and space like the rest of us—just bigger.

We do not share the cosmology of Jesus, the biblical writers, or most of human history. Our heavens are not theirs. That means, when I want to speak of God or Jesus in relation to the "heavens," I need to boldly go where no one has gone before. I need to enter the realm of imagination, not formulaic certainty. I *need* my imagination when asking what God is like in light of the universe as we know it. My eyes and ears will not take me where I need to go, nor will I find verses in the Bible that make sense of all this. I am left only to wonder and search for adequate language knowing that I will find none.

This is no meaningless, abstract exercise. At stake for me is the intelligibility of the Christian faith to myself and to those around me living in a time so utterly different from when the Christian faith took root and grew. To unleash our imaginations to speak of God is not to float adrift in unbelief, but to forge by the sweat of our brows a connection between two very different conceptions of reality. The thought of it all stuns me into silence in the face of the divine mystery, and letting the dust settle on that realization is more intelligible and comforting to me than trying to force the square peg of the current cosmos into the round hole of an ancient text.

Only our imaginations can "incite and support the eternal," to ponder the Creator we want to know amid a creation we cannot comprehend. "Faith is the assurance of things hoped for, the conviction of things not seen [Heb 11:1], and its eye is the religious imagination,"[6] as Wordsworth noted. The universe—which Christians believe God created—is declaring perhaps not so much God's glory (wow, look at that!) as God's incomprehensible mystery (uh, what?), challenging us to never mistake our limited understanding of God for God.

Yes, I find the universe—what I know of it, which is still only a fraction of a hint of a glance—unnerving, and bringing God into the picture doesn't help without some serious wrestling with what this God is all about, and, like Jacob, not letting go until I get some sort of blessing, however minimal. And unlike my own personal blown elbow incident or taxi ride crisis, the universe is a cosmic curveball that all people of faith need to adjust to—Christian, Jewish, Muslim, and others who believe in a personal God.

I am compelled to seek God anew—a God who is not utterly out of sync with the cosmos I live in, even if I stumble over my words at the very thought of it; a God who can help me make sense of the universe I live in rather than becoming a problem that needs explaining.

In the book of Romans, Paul says that God's "eternal power and divine nature . . . have been understood and seen through the things he has made" (Rom 1:20), thus leaving humanity without an excuse for worshiping God. I am not sure Paul's argument would work quite as well today, at least not without some rephrasing. Our creation is a cosmic curveball that challenges the notions of God we are familiar with rather than confirming them. If we hope to echo Paul's words today, we need a Creator God who outmatches the expansive, dynamic creation—a Creator who out-mysteries the mystery of the creation.

Adjusting to an Infinite Universe

As I mentioned earlier, I am not trying to prove, or disprove, God on the basis of science, both of which are common pitfalls on the part of Christian apologists and Christianity's cultured despisers. Rather, I am asking what kind of God are we talking about, given what we know about what this God has created. And my answer to that question has over the years slowly warmed up to the idea that God is further beyond my knowing than I might have thought.

Of course, only the most deluded among us would think they have figured God out, and both Judaism and Christianity teach that God cannot be fully known. But the heat has been turned up on the question. For much of Jewish and Christian history, the cosmos was thought to be more or less stable and fixed, that which God created "in the beginning" and forever shall be until the end of time. That universe was at least in principle a remotely graspable factor attesting to God's power.

But that stability and graspability have evaporated over the past hundred years or so. The size of the cosmos is one of the reasons why. A related reason is that the cosmos is not fixed or stable, but growing and moving in a persistent creative state, as it were, the full scope of which could not have been realized until fairly recently. Stars and galaxies are still forming, and space has been expanding since the Big Bang. The cosmos is not fixed but evolving. The days of creation in Genesis 1 continue.

Pondering the cosmos has been a big curveball for me personally, but this curveball is, as I said, one that affects us all. The cosmos has thrown us all a curveball, coming at us at light speed and from a distance of light-years, leaving us wondering whether the Creator we thought we knew so well can be comprehended at all. The God question has become more complicated, and serious theologians have taken the challenge head on.[7]

The adjustments we face today are of a different kind from what people of faith had to process in centuries past. This drives home to me the necessity of bringing science and faith into meaningful conversation. After all, we are talking about the very nature of reality, and not literal blown elbows or even the pressing questions that have been with us ever since humankind started thinking about a Higher Power, like why a good God allows evil and suffering. Now, on top of that very legitimate question, we are faced with a God who is far more mysterious and "other" than in centuries past. The God we have always looked to help us comprehend meaning has become more incomprehensible.

For me, moving forward means deliberately pressing beyond the God I was familiar with. I do not mean closing the door on the God of my youth and starting from scratch. As I said earlier, making adjustments to our understanding of God is by definition not starting over. The real question is what kind of adjustments to make, which is the heart of where the wrestling happens. That wrestling can certainly be uncomfortable, tiring, threatening, and can even feel defeating at times, but it has also given me great comfort to know that the God of all this does not have to be comprehended or brought under my control. I can face the universe around me with curiosity rather than fear. The alternate path, that our understanding of the Creator can carry on as before, is simply an unholy alliance with the limitations of human thought. I find that unthinkable.

If I may echo affirmingly Psalm 19, creation *does* leave imprints of God by which we can see God's handiwork. It's just that God's handiwork is far more bizarre and beyond us than humans have ever remotely imagined. And those imprints have driven me to reflect on what I mean when I say "God" as I am seeking, in the wonderful phrase of research psychologist Peter Todd, a "third millennium theology"[8]—an understanding of God that accounts for our image of the heavens just as all previous theologies have done for theirs.

As for me, I've made several adjustments to how I view God—not necessarily final ones, but more like warm-up swings before I step up to the plate. I'm tossing up some trial balloons in my mind's eye and seeing where they land. I believe God understands and that I have the freedom to do so.

One big adjustment concerns the Bible itself. An infinite cosmos has pushed me to own deep in the marrow of my being how pervasively the Bible's God-talk reflects the ancient world of the biblical authors. I had already been thinking about this since seminary and graduate school, but somehow I was able to keep this disruptive idea from fully penetrating my wooden skull. Then, some years back (about ten I'd say), something suddenly clicked when I stumbled upon a section of the universe dubbed the Pillars of Creation, a famous Hubble Space Telescope image of a massive cloud of dust and gas that gives birth to stars.[9] This star nursery is about sixty-five hundred light-years from us, and the largest of the "pillars" is about four light-years long.

That photo is so beautiful (and even more stunning is the image taken by the James Webb Space Telescope), yet the Pillars of Creation are just one small segment of the Eagle Nebula, which spans seventy by fifty-five light-years. I was struck by how much inconceivable beauty and wonder were waiting to be discovered out there, and the immensity of it all that reminds us that we never will. The puniness of my brief existence just clicked, and I was awakened to Pascal's loss of self.

This experience of me in front of my MacBook brought home how inadequate my thinking of God was. What the Bible and my tradition had to say about God had always been presented to me as a series of nonnegotiable, absolute truths, the immovable beginning point of all faithful theologizing, a first line of defense to make sure we are not simply caving in to the culture around us by making God in our image. The Bible and the Bible alone is suited to tell us what God is like.

It and it alone holds in check our fleeting and unreliable experiences, Hubble and James Webb Space Telescopes be damned.

I understand what motivates such claims, namely, the desire to hold fast to the "faith of our fathers," as the old hymn puts it. But once the immensity of the cosmos clicked for me, there was no making believe it didn't. Maintaining a stubborn, steely gaze against any adjustments in our understanding of God as a mark of strong faith now seemed like a recipe for disconnecting God and the world—like a rocket booster that gets ejected once the ship leaves the Earth's gravitational pull. A God who does not connect to the world around us is a God who cannot speak to us. Believing in a God who demands that we continue to adopt only biblically ancient ways of thinking of God, *which are themselves rooted in their own cultural moment,* is to diminish God's active Presence here and now. This is what I believe.

I understand the pitfalls of adjusting our theology to every fad and half-baked idea people come up with. But that does not mean that faithfulness is simply a matter of sanctifying the God-talk of, say, late medieval Europe or Iron Age Israel and being done with it. As we've seen, it has always been the way, from biblical times and throughout history, that those who seek God speak of God in ways drawn from *their* time and place. God has always been linked to the world in which God's worshipers lived and breathed. For God to be our God, that same linkage is required. For God to be intelligible to believers and broader culture, we are obligated to embrace our sacred responsibility of finding language that consciously respects the broad and ancient Christian tradition while at the same time pushing beyond it—which is to say, to embrace the wrestling match.

I firmly believe that how we make God intelligible today cannot rest simply on how others made God intelligible yesterday. As the universe continues to expand beyond our imaginations, so too must our understanding of God.

God-Talk

Speaking of other adjustments, it has become very hard for me to think of God as a "being" whose "existence" is open to rational proof or disproof. Embracing this has become critical for my spiritual sanity. From where I sit, I cannot fathom that any God worthy of the title can "exist" in the same way other "things" exist that are subject to rational proof or disproof. As I see it, if there truly is a God, this God's "existence" has to be different from what we mean by "existence" for any other *thing*. Otherwise, we are not talking about God at all, but a "being" who "exists" in the way everything else does. I do not believe we can point to evidence for God's existence as we would evidence for binary stars, black holes, or the ozone layer without tossing the idea of God entirely out the window.

I believe God's "existence" has to be spoken of differently, and this is where words fail us. As people far more insightful than I have pointed out, God is not "a being," but more like the ground of all being, the fountain of being, Being itself, or the energy that pulses through all matter.[10] I realize all this verbiage is as clear as a bodily discharge, but that is somewhat the point: the universe helps me see that when we talk about God, we are talking about that which is not like *anything*, a God who is truly far, far beyond our rational capabilities. Perhaps it's not supposed to be easy. To prove or disprove the existence of the Creator of the infinite mystery of the cosmos by means of evidence we can grasp is to confuse the Creator with the creation—which the Bible calls idolatry.

The problem we all face, however (and you probably noticed it already), is that all our language of God has to be humanized, brought down to our level, the only level we operate on, or we would not be able to say anything at all—and so I keep talking about God as a "being" with "existence" in the same breath that I say God is not a "being" who "exists." And this brings me to a core lesson I have learned in my wrestling with the cosmos: *Our language about God is metaphorical, an approximation of the Mystery of Mysteries, that will always elude our vocabulary and comprehension.*

The language we use about God and the thoughts of God we hold are adequate for communing with God and each other. Our language and thoughts should even be cherished, but with the expectation that they will and must change as we grow and have more insight. As I experienced in that San Francisco taxi, what I thought I knew about God, though adequate and reassuring for a time, turned out to be exposed as not-knowing. Admitting as much is the beginning of what it meant for me to truly believe.

Contemplating what I mean by God in our ninety-three-billion-light-year-diameter universe has also raised for me other big questions that I have been coming to peace with—which means I am learning to allow the mystery to reign in my life rather than my need to know. For instance, I think a lot about what it means to die and what happens to us afterward. To the best of my self-understanding, I am neither obsessed with nor frightened about it. I'm more restlessly curious. If heaven is a place "where we go when we die," it is not the kind of place that it has been thought to be for most of us who are encultured in Christian thinking. Perhaps heaven is just an old term for another dimension entirely? A parallel universe? I have no idea, really, and I'm fine with it. My point is simply that, as we stare into the infinite void, any conventional sense of going *up* to heaven and God looking *down* seems unlikely. We will come back to the topic of death in Chapter 11.

The universe also raises the urgency of a question that first popped up for me in my graduate school years and then twenty years later once again in the taxi: Is God only for a few, or for everyone? When I consider the endless reaches of space, the countless stars, and likely count-less orbiting plants (no doubt many containing life), it is hard for me to think that this God is all about drawing nationalistic and religious lines among the human species—even though Christian history and a fair amount of the biblical tradition have done just that. Without connecting all the dots at this moment, it seems to me that, if there is a God, this God would be love itself and not favor one people over others or condone (let alone promote) tribal hostilities.

In my experience, it seems that much (not all!) of the history of Christianity has been about exclusion to preserve a pure remnant, but in my estimation, that view of God is easier to come up with when the small, ancient Mediterranean world was the focus of attention, and without the bothersome cosmos decentering our planet and, along with it, sending all of us into obscurity. A cosmos as big as ours needs a God to match it, and I cannot imagine this God being caught up in boundary disputes, warfare bent on extermination, or other things that would divide humanity into groups rather than unite them.

The God whom the cosmos drives me toward is less "you must not let anything that breathes remain alive" (Deut 20:16) and more "For this reason I bow my knees before the Father, from whom every family in heaven and on earth takes its name" (Eph 3:14–15).

The universe has brought me to believe more deliberately that God is Spirit and is present in every atom and subatomic particle in the cosmos—in every person, every creature, and every life-form. God is ever-present, ever-creating anew, and guiding the cosmos to a goal, in which all of creation will be renewed and take part. Of course, I can prove none of this. Neither am I suggesting I've figured it out. But that is where I am at this point in my life, and it departs from what I had thought by default for years prior. This is the God I imagine, the God I have chosen to believe in even as I grasp for words to try to say any-thing coherent about God, whose imprint can be seen in the incalculable cosmos above while also being cloaked in mystery reaching farther than the cosmos itself, where even billions and trillions of light-years are dwarfed by the divine.

And in light of that, the heart of the Christian faith—the profound mystery of the incarnation, that God walked among us in human form—takes on new meaning. No one has ever understood that, and I would say that it hasn't gotten any easier for us when the very idea of God has gotten so much more out of our ability to grasp. And yet, the God of the infinite spaces is also the God of Bethlehem and Calvary; the God of infinite power is also the God who aligns with the humiliating death of Roman crucifixion. In Jesus as well, we see paradoxically something of the face of an incomprehensible yet vulnerable God.

Christianity is an odd religion, indeed. And pondering the immense paradox of the God of the cosmos dwelling in human form makes me want to stay in my own lane. I find myself more and more turning my gaze away from trying to grasp the God of the very large things to something I at least have a shot at addressing—my own thoughts and actions toward others.

God is not simply "great." God is mystery, a mystery I am invited to respond to. Perhaps that is the best way of summing up the universe's effect on my thinking about God. And, lo and behold, here and there the Bible has a few things to say about this kind of God, too.

Chapter 6

Just When You Thought
You Had the Bible Figured Out

AS CRUEL FATE would have it, I am a college Bible professor. I therefore get a lot of questions from students who
were taught to think of the Bible as a fairly straightforward
source of information directly from God for what to believe and
how to live—which works pretty well until you start getting into
the details.

The truth is, the Bible can be a tough read. After all, by the time
we get to chapter 6 of the Bible (in the book of Genesis), pretty
much everyone drowns because the Creator has apparently run out
of patience and ideas. Many of my students have never really taken
in the Noah story and are shocked at what they find when we read it
together. Others are looking for deeper answers than the images of
smiling giraffes, elephants, and bunnies boarding the ark. They want
to understand how this short-tempered feudal overlord can be the
same God who "so loved the world" in John's Gospel. God is often
portrayed in the Bible as violent—not everywhere, to be sure, but
enough times that we can't just brush it aside like a pesky mosquito.

Year in and year out, this has been the issue my students have most wanted to talk about.

The Bible also presents other problems for attentive and curious readers, such as whole sections that are, frankly, not only tough to slog through but seem meaningful only to the narrow band of ancient humans for whom these sections were originally written. Whole books are dedicated to the rise and disastrous fall of Israel's monarchy, where the main lesson seems to be, "Well that went horribly, here's why, and let's remember not to repeat this in the future." Are sleep-deprived new mothers expected to schlep through all this just because "it's in the Bible"? Even the laws, which are so central to the Hebrew Bible, are often hard to relate to, because they typically assume an ancient setting—like how to treat slaves and virgin daughters, what to do with livestock that don't stay on their side of the fence, and what animals are to be sacrificed in certain situations. Anyone living at some other point in time than the ancient writers (which is everyone else) has had to engage in some creative readings of these laws to coax them into a time and place for which they were never intended.

My point, if my experience in teaching and speaking on the subject is worth anything, is that many people of faith are not so interested in panning the Bible for hours and hours for a few flecks of gold. I am not at all surprised to see people stop reading it entirely, and even lose interest in any faith system built upon it.

I get it. I really do. And so do the Christians and Jews who have been struggling with these things for as long as there has been a Bible.[1] But we are in a different place today in the history of Judaism and Christianity. On top of all the other issues people have had with the Bible, we now are faced with a universe where the very fabric of reality is up for grabs. The Bible seems out of touch. How Christians today can connect with this ancient Bible is a more pressing question than it has ever been. Adjustments have to be made.

And with that, here is something about the Bible I found surprising once I actually saw it. You might find it surprising too, because it doesn't get the airtime it deserves: *the Bible invites its readers to embrace the mystery of God, the kind of mystery that our lives and the universe we live in demand of us if we want to continue to be people of faith.*

The Bible most certainly talks about God in ways that made sense in ancient times—there is no use making believe otherwise. But the biblical writers also catch glimpses of a God who goes far beyond their—or anybody's—reckoning. These are the parts of the Bible that have risen to the surface for me; they have helped me to continue the conversation of faith between an ancient tradition and our radically different modern world.

Mystery helps tie my world to that of the biblical writers.

The truth is, I read the Bible for decades without seeing what we might call its "mystery passages." I noticed them, of course, but would pause only long enough to remark, "Gee, that's interesting and weird," and then move along my merry way. I didn't see—better, couldn't see—these mystery passages until I had to . . . until I was ready. It took times of disorientation, when everything was falling apart for me—intellectually, personally, spiritually—when I was searching for ways to keep it together and to see the bigger picture of faith. And the more I thought about the routine biblical story as it was taught to me, the more it felt out of place and hugely unhelpful to me spiritually. When you're dealing with an infinite universe and the Bible you want to take seriously doesn't acknowledge said universe, you've got what's called a theological problem. I had to address that problem, not ignore it—and make adjustments to my understanding of God vis-à-vis the universe where needed.

That's when I began letting in those parts of the Bible I had been breezing over in years past. Now a floodlight was shining on them. I was now ready to see them . . . because I needed to.

Revisiting an Old Friend

Remember Psalm 19? As I said, the "heavens" that this writer wrote about—the heavens that show us God's glory—are ancient heavens, devoid of images from space telescopes and million-plus light-year distances. And so, even though the heavens led this ancient author to praise, our heavens led me, and others, like Blaise Pascal, to a disorienting crisis of faith.

But there is one vital way that we do indeed connect with this ancient writer: what is out there in the heavens should elicit in us a sense of awe—or as biblical writers tend to put it, the "fear of the Lord." In that much at least we are akin to our psalm writer: the cosmos drives us to say something about God, and that something should be laced with a healthy dose of awe *because of what we observe around us.*

The difference, as I've been saying, is that the psalmist's God-talk fits well with his heavens and not ours (remember his cosmos has a dome overhead), but the principle is the same for both ancient and modern pilgrims of faith: the big sky above is telling us something about God. But filling in the gap of what that something is, it seems to me, *must* be adjusted as our knowledge of the heavens is adjusted.

Another thing that is striking about Psalm 19 is that the author's knowledge of the heavens didn't come to him by means of a divine memo. The notion of a dome bowing across the expanse above is not an Israelite invention; we see similar notions expressed in other religious traditions that are considerably older than Israel's. In fact, as scholars of antiquity generally agree, Israel's notion of the heavens is in no small way dependent on how everyone else back then—such as Egyptians, Babylonians, and Canaanites—thought about what lay above. The ancient myths all seemed to breathe the same air when it came to explaining what was going on high above, even if they differed in many details.

My point here is that the ancient Israelites accepted the common ways of explaining the cosmos in their day—let's call those explanations the "science" of the day. They modified those common explanations to reflect their specific beliefs and committed them to writing.

I can't help but think there is a lesson here to be learned for people of faith today.

Had the ancient Israelites not adopted agreed-upon notions of the cosmos, their God-talk would have fallen on deaf ears. Had they simply made up their own story with no connection to the common knowledge of the time, they would have been whispering into a hurricane. So, too, if we wish to speak of God meaningfully, in ways that engage the people of today, we cannot do so by forcing them to swallow an ancient reality that is demonstrably not real. We have to work with the science we have *as they did with theirs* and find words to talk about this God that show awareness of our cosmos.

Another psalm that captures this vibe is Psalm 104. In this lengthy and rich poem, God is praised over and over again for the works of creation, taking its readers back to the very dawn of time when the heavens, earth, waters, vegetation, and creatures were fashioned. It also echoes closely a much older Egyptian hymn to the sun god Aten. Here again, the biblical writer's view of creation was not his invention but part of his broader social and religious context—and he is praising the God of *Israel* nonetheless.

The Israelites believed that God is revealed in every corner of creation and that true awareness of creation leads to amazement and praise of God. Theologian Abraham Heschel remarks, "wonder or radical amazement, the state of maladjustment to words and notions,[2] is therefore a prerequisite for an authentic awareness of that which is." Maladjustment to words and notions. I love that phrase. That's pretty deep, and probably worth reading once or twice more. As one of my doctoral professors, Jon Levenson, puts it, building off of Heschel's comment, the goal of Psalm 104 (and the hymn to Aten), "is to evoke this experience [of awe] by shocking us out of our familiarity with the natural order in which we find ourselves, by confronting us with the perpetual newness of nature and its humbling oddness."

Today our cosmos is also "shocking us out of our familiarity" with the "newness of nature and its humbling oddness," but like never before. I think ancient people, even though they had a much smaller cosmos to deal with, had a sense of nature's grandeur that we do not have. We in the modern West have been all about conquering nature and isolating ourselves from it (by artificial lights and living indoors) rather than learning from it. As a result we are left with a very small god who acts (if at all) according to our own limiting conceptions of reality.[3]

By trying to control our world, we have deluded ourselves into thinking that we control the Creator. Facing the infinite cosmos rids us of this childish delusion. Thank you, science.

One more thing: the world that our ancient authors saw pointed them to a God they could not see, and back to a time they did not experience—the dawn of creation. This is exactly the role that modern cosmology can play for those who are seeking a deeper sense of the Creator. Pascal's "eternal silence of the infinite spaces" is likewise pointing us to a God whose . . . bigness, grandeur, omnipresence—words fail me . . . match that experienced reality. We do not comprehend but can only trust that our heavens, as it was for the psalmist, are declaring for us the glory of God. And that glory is as far from our understanding as are the distant galaxies that swirl about in the infinite expanses of the universe.

God is, if anything, mystery. And yet, that mystery is, as the Christian faith claims, alive in and around us, and particularly present in

Jesus of Nazareth. That meeting of infinite reality in a finite human is perhaps the grandest mystery of the Christian tradition, a notion that I find both incomprehensible and comforting.

Paul the Mystic

Paul tends to get a bad rap, mainly because of how he's been enlisted in our time to give "biblical support" to all sorts of things Paul, as an ancient man, probably wouldn't have known what to do with. There is much more to Paul than a collection of prooftexts for our personal agendas. Paul was actually a pretty deep guy, and as one who claimed to have been "caught up to the third heaven" (2 Cor 12:2), he had a view of God that I believe rises above our tribal squabbles. One place to see Paul breaking through mundane reality is in the book of Colossians, which is not a book at all but a short letter written to the Roman colony of Colossae in what was once called Asia Minor (Turkey).

Having said that, I need to mention that, though this letter is attributed to Paul, many—more likely most—scholars are skeptical. Its vibe is quite different from other letters of Paul, and so scholars commonly conclude that it was written by an associate of Paul after his death. Personally, I'm not completely sold on this hunch. I think it's possible Paul could have written letters with multiple vibes. After all, don't we all communicate differently depending on the audience and situation?

And yet, I find the broader scholarly arguments against Pauline authorship on the whole to be rather hefty and persuasive, though there is no need to argue the point here. Either way, there is a big payoff for us. If Paul wrote Colossians, then the different vibe could be chalked up to Paul's perspective changing over time. Colossians, in that case, would show us an elder, more contemplative Paul compared with some of his earlier writings, which some would call overly doctrinaire or combative (see 1 Thessalonians or Galatians). If, however, Colossians was written after Paul's death, then it reflects the view of one or more people close to Paul who developed Paul's thinking in directions Paul himself had not.

I get excited about this second (and seemingly more likely) option, because it serves as a snapshot of the main theme of this book: *adjusting our understanding of God according to the experiences that befall us.* I take Colossians to be a very early example in the Christian faith of a later generation adapting the voice of their late, revered teacher to address things that he had not addressed. After Paul's death around 63 CE, others, no doubt indebted to Paul, picked up his mantle and wrote a letter to Colossae, a community Paul had founded, taking on Paul's persona. And what we find in this letter is a way of speaking of faith in Christ that takes on a mystical bent.

I do not mean some sort of esoteric, secret knowledge meant only for a select few with their heads in the clouds. I am using "mystical" to mean an immediate experience of spiritual reality that cannot be fully articulated by words nor captured by analytical means. To borrow Paul's words from elsewhere, the experience of God's Presence "passes all understanding." This sort of immediate and ongoing experience of Christ is available to all, a point about which the community at Colossae might need some reminding now that their spiritual father is dead. Paul is gone, but the Christ is as near to them as ever. I think that is the author's point.

I've been very moved over the years by this letter, even if I do not always feel I adequately understand it—though *not* understanding seems appropriate. Colossians points us to the mystery of God, gives us glimpses of a higher plane, nudges us beyond our mundane experience to recognize that the reality of God will not be boxed up in our perceived reality.

One line in this letter moves me to stillness: In Christ "are hidden all the treasures of wisdom and knowledge" (Col 2:3). I have at home a decorative tile from my German grandmother (of blessed memory) with these words painted on it. I keep it just off to the side of my computer screen to make sure it catches my eye now and then. It is worth letting every word simmer.

Wisdom and knowledge are treasures that are hidden in Christ. Catching only a glimpse of this, I ask myself, "What if this is true?" And who is this "Christ"? Does he mean the Jesus who walked around on earth, or the raised and gone-to-heaven Jesus? I don't think so. More likely this is the cosmic, universal Christ, who, according to John's Gospel, is the "Word" who predates creation and through whom all things exist. As we will see later, this Christ is deeply enmeshed in the universe itself and was also made flesh two thousand years ago. Whichever way we parse it, "Christ" is not simply a synonym of "Jesus of Nazareth." And even though "Christ" is used in the Gospels to mean "Messiah" in the conventional Jewish sense (a liberating king), in Christian circles it would come to mean more. Colossians 2:3 is hinting at that deeper, more mystical meaning.

And remember that this letter, like all of the New Testament letters, is not a tract to convert the unconverted but was written to a community of Jesus followers. The treasures of wisdom and knowledge are hidden *for them* as pilgrims of faith, not from them. They are invited to enter into deeper communion with God through Christ, where wisdom and knowledge are limitless.

The words "all" and "hidden" stand out to me. There is so much more—infinitely more—to the knowledge of God than what we can understand. Much in the same way the universe is hidden from our perception, God is far more than we perceive God to be. All of our theologies, no matter how robust we claim them to be, never grasp the all-ness and hiddenness of wisdom and knowledge. Some can be known, but not all. How could we think otherwise?[4]

A few sentences earlier (Col 1:24), we find a rather bewildering comment. A common thread throughout Paul's letters concerns suffering, which forges a mystical communion with Christ. In the letter to the Philippians, Paul writes that "sharing" both Christ's sufferings and his death are what it means to "know" Christ. But Colossians goes a step further: the imprisoned writer rejoices because "in my flesh I am completing what is lacking in Christ's afflictions for the sake of his body, that is, the church."

I don't understand what it means for Christ's afflictions to be "lacking" or the writer's claim to be "completing" them—and I don't recall ever hearing anyone in church or seminary explain it. It seems to me that, in his suffering, this writer sees himself as not just mimicking Jesus or following his example, but "being" Christ for the sake of the church. I can imagine a speedy heresy trial in some circles today if someone were to hint at such an idea, but there you have it, right there in the Bible.

I don't think the writer intends this to be understood as a one-off brag, but as a pattern of living for his readers. Christ's sufferings continue, as it were, through his followers for the benefit of others. When they suffer, they *are* Christ to others. It seems like Christ's sufferings were—again, in some sense I cannot grasp—not enough, lacking, since others will come along at a later time and wonder how they, too, can be connected to the suffering Christ of history. The answer is that the suffering of others fills up this lack and benefits the whole.

We are certainly in the realm of true mystery here—a cosmic, transrational glimpse of the interconnectedness of Christ, his followers, and God that lifts us above the commonplace reality we perceive. The insight of this passage is not meant to be understood but experienced. It is not meant to be controlled but accepted.

Similarly, a bit later, we read, "you have been raised with Christ" (Col 3:1). This is no flowery turn of phrase, but a grasping for language to express a deep mystery. One does not simply "follow" Christ as if two steps behind. Rather, one is . . . how can we put it? . . . grafted into Christ, so much so that followers of Jesus can be spoken of as having *already* been raised *with* Christ. This raising is not physical (of course), but participating in a new spiritual dimension, as it were. And as such, "your life is [now] hidden with Christ in God" (Col 3:3). Most of my life I have perceived how casually we Christians sometimes speak of "becoming a Christian." For the early followers of Jesus, however, it meant a mystical participation in the central mysteries of the suffering, death, and resurrection of the Son of God.

And this same Christ is the one in whom—as we read earlier in the letter—"all things in heaven and on earth were created, things visible and invisible, whether thrones or dominions or rulers or powers—all things have been created through him and for him. He himself is before all things, and in him all things hold together" (Col 1:16–17).

Here too the nuances are challenging to tease out, but Christ is, in a word, foundational to and prior to the cosmos itself (much like we read in the beginning of John's Gospel, likewise written several decades after the time of Jesus). Christ's followers are intertwined with this cosmic Christ, the Christ of heaven and earth, of all things visible and invisible, the Christ in whom all things—the infinite cosmos—hold together. According to this ancient writer, being a follower of Jesus means being invited into the mystery of the cosmos and of all there is, and which we by definition cannot grasp.

Throughout all the letters attributed to Paul, the language most often used to speak to this mystical reality is being "in Christ." (Be on the lookout, too, for "into Christ," "with Christ," and occasionally "Christ in you.") Another way of putting it is that believers are "united" with Christ, as Paul writes in the letter to the Romans. This kind of language defies description. It is intimate, and it makes "accepting" Jesus, or "making a faith commitment," sound aridly clinical by comparison. Paul is not satisfied to describe the mechanics of faith. He is groping for language to describe being caught up in mystery.

We are skimming the surface, but even glimpsing these sorts of overtures in the letters attributed to Paul has helped me look at God and the nature of faith differently from what I had grown accustomed to. The gospel points to a transcendent reality that cannot be articulated according to the conceptions of the present humdrum reality. This has been helpful for me to remember as I try to navigate my life of faith in face of an infinitely large universe. Paul and his followers, in their own way and in their own time, were—thankfully—already placing the Christian faith in the realm of mystery.

Don't Forget John. John Is Huge.

The Gospel of John and the three letters of John sound a similar note to Paul's letters. These New Testament books are, like most biblical books, anonymous. No author is ascribed; we don't know who wrote them or even if the same person wrote all or some of them. Calling the author John is a matter of church tradition. What does seem to be clear to most biblical scholars, however, is that the Gospel of John and the letters were written somewhat later than most of the other New Testament books. They were addressing a later generation of Jesus followers, and their message was shaped to speak into their circumstances.

To give one example, toward the end of the Gospel of John, Thomas the doubting disciple comes to believe that Jesus is raised in the flesh only because he saw Jesus's wounds with his own eyes. Jesus said to Thomas, "Have you believed because you have seen me? Blessed are those who have not seen and yet have come to believe" (John 20:29). Of the four Gospels, only John includes this scene, which seems to be aimed at reassuring his readers, who had not experienced Jesus, that they too could believe. John's Gospel is asking what happens to the Jesus movement as one generation gives way to the next and then the next. The answer is that they who believe without seeing are nevertheless blessed by Jesus himself.

John's Gospel also emphasizes a deep spiritual intimacy similar to what we see in the letters of Paul. In chapter 17, just before his arrest and crucifixion, Jesus prays for his disciples for the courage they will need as they go out and spread the word amid opposition. And then Jesus says this:

> I ask not only on behalf of these, but also on behalf of those who will believe in me through their word, that they may all be one. As you, Father, are in me and I am in you, may they also be in us, so that the world may believe that you have sent me. The glory that you have given me I have given them, *so that they may be one, as we are one, I in them and you in me, that they may become completely one*, so that the world may know that you have sent me and have loved them even as you have loved me. (John 17:20–23; italics added)

It's easy to get lost in the repetitiveness, a typical feature of John's Gospel, but here is the point, as far as I can see. While praying for the disciples, Jesus is also praying for those who *will* believe. As with the Doubting Thomas story, this prayer homes in on those who are far removed from Jesus of Nazareth. God is with them, too—in a mystical way. The intimacy that the Father shares with the Son—an unfathomable mystery in its own right—is the same intimacy that is to be shared with those who believe regardless of whether they have seen Jesus for themselves. And so, later believers also take part in the divine intimacy, where they become one with God and with each other. As John writes more succinctly (but not more clearly) a bit earlier, "I am in my Father, and you in me, and I in you" (John 14:20).

Let me add briefly two more comments from John's Gospel that are familiar and for that reason not always appreciated as they deserve. Jesus says, "*I am* the way, and the truth, and the life" (John 14:6, emphasis added) and not "beliefs about me are the way and the truth and the life." In Jesus, according to John, is the way . . . truth . . . life. Jesus embodies these things. Likewise, John 3:16, "For God so loved the world that he gave his only Son," says more than God gave Earth a care package. Rather, God in Christ chose to experience the world. We'll get more into the importance of "God with us" a bit later in the book, but for now it strikes me that the mystery of the Creator experiencing the creation deserves more than the passing glance it often gets.

John's Gospel presents a vision of what it means to "believe"—entering into the divine mystery, a union of love that transcends our mortal limitations, a state so profound it is no wonder early Christian mystics like John of the Cross (1542–1591) and Teresa of Ávila (1515–1582) waxed poetic about it, even if we have forgotten how.

I have come to think, as have so many others in the course of history, that the goal of Christian faith is the *experience* of God, not the comprehension of God.[5] It saddens—better, frustrates—me to reflect on some of my earlier Christian influences, where my personal experience was not simply sidelined but vilified as subjective and even sinful, something that should by all means *never* be trusted. At best, experience should take a back seat to analysis, to internalizing carefully scripted theological formulas that brought God down to earth rather than lifting us up above it. But a central theme of this book is that experiences matter, and John's Gospel points his late generation readers to the experience of God, which we desperately need to be pointed to as well.

The cosmos around us makes God seem less friendly to our rational capabilities, not more. That is actually good news, for if we choose to listen, the creation will point us toward relinquishing the illusion of intellectual control and seeking instead what we truly need: the intimacy that John and Paul hint at, an intimacy that can only be experienced.

Becoming Divine

Like Colossians and John's Gospel, 2 Peter is another New Testament book that was likely not written by the person who bears its name, Peter, a disciple of Jesus, but by an anonymous author living perhaps as late as the second century. A decent study Bible will lay out the reasons why modern scholars arrive at this conclusion, though scholars long before the modern period expressed serious doubts about the authorship of the letter, including big names like Origen (third century), Eusebius (fourth century), and John Calvin (sixteenth century). And once again, it seems we are dealing with a biblical writer who had in his sights those far removed from the time of Jesus, who were asking themselves, "What's in it for us? How do we connect to all of this?"

The answer this author gives is that God has gifted them with God's own divine power so that they "may escape from the corruption that is in the world . . . and may become participants of the divine nature" (2 Pet 1:4). That's quite a statement.

Like Paul's "in Christ" and John's invitation to enter divine intimacy, Peter's words are also speaking of intimacy with God, if also a bit abstractly. But that is what you get when you are trying to explain something that our everyday ways of thinking aren't equipped to handle. Among the Christian traditions, the Eastern Orthodox Church has had the most to say about this mystical, spiritual connection between us and God, which they call "theosis," or the deification of humans.

Please don't blow a gasket. The Orthodox Church is not saying humans literally become God. Rather, theosis is trying to get at a weighty spiritual reality of the Christian faith: the whole purpose of the mystery of God entering the human experience concretely in Jesus is for humans to be able to take on divinity. In other words, Christ brought together the divine and the human, and those who are "in Christ" (to use Paul's language) likewise participate in the divine nature. This way of talking goes back at least as far as the theologian Athanasius (fourth century). Some of us may recognize the idea from C. S. Lewis's writings:

> He [God] will make the feeblest and filthiest of us into a god or goddess, dazzling, radiant, immortal creatures, pulsating all through with such energy and joy and wisdom and love as we cannot now imagine, a bright stainless mirror which reflects back to Him perfectly (though, of course, on a smaller scale) His own boundless power and delight and goodness.[6]

Again, I do not claim to understand fully what 2 Peter and the other New Testament writers mean, nor are theologians always clear in explaining it. All the better, as far as I'm concerned. If I felt I had a good handle on it, I would be tempted simply to reduce this mystical reality to another thought to control. And today, perhaps more than ever, all of us could use a vision of God that we cannot control and a faith that invites us to embrace the not-knowing that mystery demands. At least I know I do.

"The creation declares the mystery of God," to rewrite Psalm 19. At least some of the biblical writers were already there, long before we were. They intuited that when it comes to God, our words are place-holders, signposts we erect along the journey as we continue forward.

I see much more is at stake here than our own individual faith journeys. As I mentioned earlier, I have come to believe that the future viability of the Christian faith depends on our willingness to adjust how we understand God, Jesus, the Bible, and the nature of faith in light of an infinite universe. To embrace the mystery of God is vital to a "third-millennium theology."

And that is the point, isn't it?—to make our faith viable, not simply for others but for ourselves. This has always been the way, from the very beginning of ancient Israelite faith to this very moment: humans have spoken of God in ways that make sense for them in the world as they understood it. In our time, our understanding of the world and the universe has changed more dramatically and more quickly than at any other time in human history. Such rapid changes can understandably make us feel nervous and want to cling more tightly to familiar ways of thinking about God. But it is precisely because of these rapid and fundamental changes to our understanding of reality that I feel I need to adjust my understanding of God to keep pace.

The only question I, and I would suggest all of us, have is whether we will follow the path laid out before us, leave aside our various needs to micromanage the outcome, and seek afresh the divine mystery with curiosity, humility, and trust.

The universe has thrown us all a major curveball in connecting with the God of the Bible. But, as writer and pastor Mark William Worthing puts it, "If God created the physical universe, then the knowledge gained from the investigation of this universe cannot be unconnected to its Creator." That pretty much sums it all up. The Bible's embrace of mystery can help us accept this challenge.[7]

I also resonate strongly with the words of Roman Catholic theologian Karl Rahner: "The Christian of the future will be a mystic or will not be at all."[8] The more we come to know about our cosmos, the more we will need to embrace the mystery of God if we wish to have a faith that is intelligible to ourselves and to others.

Rahner, writing in the early 1960s, was responding to the rapid changes of the twentieth century, among them scientific advances. And one of those advances concerns the nature of the human story itself.

Chapter 7

The Other 99 Percent

S*MITHSONIAN MAGAZINE* recently posted an article[1] featuring the absolutely cutest little lion cub you'll ever want to see. Her name is Sparta, and you just want to hug her—were it not for the fact she's been frozen solid in the Siberian permafrost for some time, about twenty-eight thousand years. What makes this cub rank so high on the hugability scale is how well preserved she is. She looks like she's about to wake up, stretch, and headbutt you (or claw your face off).

Cave lions were a thing back during the last Ice Age, and humans drew cave pictures of them. I'm sure Sparta (or any other lion) wasn't anyone's cave pet, but seeing that picture of her lying there "sleeping" struck me how much a twenty-eight-thousand-year-old lion cub can look so at home right now. If we had well-preserved humans from so long ago, I'd be saying the same thing about them. Of course, many things separate humans today from humans thirty millennia ago. They wouldn't know what to make of our technology or why there are so many old people (older than thirty) walking around. And if I were transported back to their world, I'd probably succumb to injuries, frost, or starvation by late afternoon. But still, we'd see each other, I imagine, as fundamentally human.

These thoughts were triggered for me by coming across that photo of Sparta. If this long-dead adorable feline could look so recognizable today, I am left pondering, despite the passage of tens of thousands of years, how different are we, really, from those ancient humans who roamed the frozen earth and drew kitty pictures on cave walls.

Along those lines, my own existence seems trivial when I think about how long humans have been around doing very humanlike things. Cave art goes back at least forty thousand years. At least fifteen thousand years ago (according to commonly held opinion), ancient travelers migrated from Asia to become true Native Americans, the first settlers of the continent I currently occupy. The oldest known boat, the Pesse canoe, is about ten thousand years old, and recent evidence suggests that humans were traveling over water in boats or rafts at least seventy thousand years ago. We know from cave paintings that Mongolians held wrestling matches seven thousand years ago, when, according to the first chapter of the Bible, the cosmos was still trapped in a cosmic, primordial, chaotic ocean (aka the "Deep"). The Sumerians (in modern-day Iraq) were brewing beer six thousand years ago, around the time when the Bible says God created light.[2]

Humans have also had religious sensibilities for thousands of years, far longer than the three Abrahamic religions have been around. At an archaeological site in Turkey called Göbekli Tepe, scientists uncovered an eleven-thousand-year-old structure that many have interpreted as a temple, which would make it the oldest one known to date.[3] Whether or not this is the case, people across the globe, and with no contact with the ancient Israelites, have been worshiping some deity or deities long before the Israelites came on the scene. Stonehenge, an ancient burial site in England, also appears to have religious significance, and was built five thousand years ago, one thousand years before Abraham, Israel's first ancestor, came on the scene.

God may be beyond time, but it is easy for me to fall into the trap of thinking that my religious tradition is as well. The fact, though, is that humans have been around for eons, and for most of that time they have known nothing of the religious faiths and conceptions of God that I take for granted. The oldest of the three Abrahamic religions, Judaism, has been around for only roughly three thousand years, about 1 percent of the total time humans more or less like us have roamed the earth (about three hundred thousand years).[4] I struggle with this. I am left wondering how the other 99 percent of the human drama connects with the God I have come to accept as the one who always was. How do the "ancient" stories of my tradition (starring the relatively modern Moses, David, Jesus, and Paul) relate to a human saga that is vastly older and more complex than this tradition can account for?

In a way, I am back at Harvard or riding in the taxi in San Francisco, gripped by the question of what God truly thinks of "outsiders." Only now these outsiders are not my classmates or a lunchtime crowd walking along a city street but cover three hundred thousand years of human history. It's enough to make you just sit down and try to clear your head. What does God think about this other 99 percent? I've always heard that God has a "plan," but does that plan include the ancient architects who were driven to construct Stonehenge and Göbekli Tepe? If so, how? If not, my tradition begins to feel rather limited to the last microsecond of recent history. Does the God of Abraham look lovingly upon ancient cave drawings and temples dedicated to the only gods ancient humans could have known?

My tradition never dealt with any of this. Perhaps the signal they were unwittingly sending was that this 99 percent is just a dispensable prelude, a warm-up act, to "us," the main event, the truly special humans that God cares about. But Sparta suggests otherwise to me, as do ancient canoes, temples, and six-packs. Their humanity cannot be questioned. So, where are God and Jesus in all this?

Like the images from the Hubble and James Webb Space Telescopes, I can't ignore what the study of human history has brought to my attention. I find it curious, however, even a bit frustrating, that at least in my circles, few Christians struggle with the curveball of humanity's long, diverse, strange, yet strangely familiar saga. And the Bible is no help whatsoever in addressing my questions, and understandably so, seeing as how its writers had zero interest in, let alone knowledge of, tens of thousands of years of humanity, nor has most of Christian history. The only nod the Bible gives to the dawn of human cultures and languages (see Genesis chapters 4 and 10–11) reads precisely like Greek myth, the kind of thing we would expect ancient people to write.

Cultural anthropology, which is what we are talking about here, has challenged how I understand God's activity in the world and what it means to be human in much the same way that grappling with light speed and trillions of galaxies has. I feel that my conceptions of God are too small for working through all this—they are more an intrusion than a solution. As it turns out, I need to make adjustments, not only to account for the history of humans, but for a much more ancient, and more familiar, story. And if my experience counts for anything, I know many people of faith who have stood in the batter's box and faced down this same pitch.

THE Curveball

I have a sense about why frozen lion cubs and cave drawings of wrestling matches haven't gotten the attention they deserve: they've been crowded out by what has been perceived as a far more menacing curveball for Christian faith—evolution.

Judging by the strong reactions it has evoked, I would argue that evolution remains *the* intellectual curveball thrown at Christian faith ever since Charles Darwin popularized the theory in the nineteenth century. Evolution takes us back to a time long before the first humans, to the very dawn of single-cell life, somewhere around 3.8 billion years ago. The part of the evolutionary chain that would eventually lead to humans (namely, creatures walking on two legs) began around 2.8 million years ago. *Homo sapiens* (aka us) emerged around three hundred thousand years ago and were once one of several human species. By about fifteen to forty thousand years ago *Homo sapiens* was the only remaining human species (we won), and the rest is, quite literally, human history in all its tragedies and triumphs.[5]

This scenario is where science has had its most ugly and best-known collision with the Bible. Genesis 1 is quite clear that God created humans en masse a few thousand years ago on the sixth and final day of the creation week by simply speaking them into existence—and we've stayed the same, biologically speaking, ever since. Genesis may make distinctions between humans and other creatures of land, sea, and air, but certainly not among the human species. Genesis 2 offers another version of the creation story, one with a very different sequence. Here God created one man, Adam, out of dirt, then all the animals, and then the first woman, Eve. Having two such contradictory creation stories at the beginning of the Bible is an interesting topic in and of itself, but it won't detain us here. The main point is that the Bible leaves no room for the emergence of humans over a multimillion-year process.

So what? Well, a lot of long-cherished Christian ideas about God and the world are rooted in literal readings of the Bible. Once you bring evolution into the discussion, those ideas begin to take a big hit. For many, a lot is at stake for Christian theology if the biblical story of the creation of humans isn't at least in some sense literally true. For one thing, if God did not directly create us humans but we are one species that evolved along with all others, what makes us so special? How could humans be made in God's "image," as Genesis 1 says, touched directly by God's hand as it were, if we evolved over millions of years?

After many years of keeping this information deeply sealed in my inner vault, there came a time when I knew that I could no longer avoid this predicament. Evolution takes us from being the unique center of all of creation and puts us more at the edges, as a latecomer, deeply dependent on all that went before for us and interconnected with all life-forms. Along with the massive amounts of DNA we share with apes, cats, and other mammals, we even share about 60 percent of our DNA with bananas, 50 percent with trees, 45 percent with cabbage, and 26 percent with yeast[6]—and I will refrain from suggesting that this may well explain how some of my undergraduates manage to fail open-book tests.

The biblical story that takes the biggest hit from evolution, especially for Christians, is the story of the first couple's unfortunate act of eating the forbidden fruit. As punishment, among other things, God consigned Adam and Eve to mortality, which is said to explain how death entered the world. What turns up the heat for Christians is that this story gets picked up in the New Testament in a big way. According to the apostle Paul, Jesus is the second or new Adam. By his crucifixion and resurrection, Jesus defeated sin and death, which Adam and Eve's disobedience had introduced.

In one fell swoop, evolution wreaks havoc with this scenario. No first couple caused the world's woes because there was no first couple. Suffering and death, rather than being alien to the world, were from an evolutionary point of view a necessary part of the process all along. Death actually propels evolution forward via random genetic mutations, natural selection, and the survival of the fittest. If it weren't for this death-studded process, Christians, ironically, wouldn't even be here to ponder whether evolution is true.

Evolution was the proverbial bombshell that dropped on the quiet countryside of Christian (and to a lesser extent, Jewish) faith. It *had* to be addressed somehow, and Christians have done so in basically three ways: (1) by rejecting evolution and sticking with a literal reading of Genesis, (2) by jury-rigging scenarios in which evolution and a literal (or semiliteral) reading of Genesis can coexist, and (3) by changing how we think about Genesis and God in light of the impact of evolution.

It probably won't come as a shock that I am very much of the third option and not a fan of the first two. I would argue, in fact, that the third option is actually more faithful to the biblical tradition than the other two options, because it recognizes, with Paul, that God is revealed in creation (see Rom 1:19–20). It is the only option that makes space for our experience of the world around us.

Concerning the first option, I feel I am in absolutely no position to reject a widely held theory like evolution on the basis of whether or not I like it. I am not trained in the field, and I gladly assume that evolutionary scientists are perpetrating no conspiracy, nor are they utterly incompetent or self-deluded. I am not scientifically trained, and I have to rely on those who are, which includes committed Jews and Christians. I am no more equipped to debate the fossil record or genetic evidence for evolution than I am to debate how quickly a distant galaxy is moving away from us.

Furthermore, as a biblical scholar, I find that the story of Adam and Eve on its own terms does not read like literal history when compared with other ancient creation stories of the time. In fact, I think the ancient Israelites were quite intent on letting their readers know that the story is not history, seeing as it includes a talking serpent and two magic-like trees. The story is screaming to us, "Please read me symbolically, metaphorically, theologically—anything but literally!"

The second option mentioned above seems promising for some,

and it comes from a genuine desire to accept evolution and retain a literal Adam *in some sense*. But for me, melding together evolution and a literal Adam and Eve, in any sense, is a forced explanation. It is driven neither by our understanding of the science nor by the ancient context of Genesis, but by a need to preserve the Bible's spiritual authority. Sure, evolution is true, but finding a "literal historical Adam" in some sense—*any* sense—is thought to preserve "biblical authority" while also allowing evangelicals to work with the science.

For my tastes, this have-your-cake-and-eat-it-too scenario creates more problems than it solves. It treats evolution not as an all-encompassing theory with sweeping explanatory power about *all* life (not just human life), but more as an unfortunate irritation that has to be made to fit with the Bible. Squeezing the biblical Adam into an evolution framework also yields some hybrid solutions that appear desperate to me. For example, genetic data suggest that modern humans are descended not from a first couple but from a gene pool of a few thousand humans living about one hundred thousand years ago. Hence, a "historical Adam" is reframed as a first gene pool. Others say Adam and Eve were an actual couple of one of the common ancestors of *Homo sapiens*.[7] In either scenario, both evolution and the direct "creation" of a first human couple are said to be preserved—at least that is the plan.

I have never been drawn to square-peg-in-round-hole ad hoc arguments like these. They exist to preserve the perceived doctrinal necesssity of the historical nature of the Adam and Eve story. It seems self-defeating to defend biblical literalism by making "Adam" into something—a gene pool or caveman—that the Bible doesn't remotely leave room for.

And this brings me to my point. As different as options 1 and 2 are in temperament, they share the same problem: both treat their understanding of God as a given, a certainty, something settled and immovable. The new thing, evolution, either needs to be ignored or simply grafted onto existing views of God—like pinning the evolutionary tail on the biblical donkey.

But what if evolution is alerting us that we need an understanding of God that makes sense in view of the whole shebang of evolution?

I have made my home in the third option listed above, for reasons that echo what I said about the cosmos in Chapter 5. Scientific discoveries of the physical world shape how we think about God—not impulsively, not willy-nilly, but thoughtfully and in community. This leads me to consider seriously that evolution is the Creator's way of creating. To paraphrase Psalm 19 yet again, "What we have learned about the evolution of life declares the glory of God." If God is Creator, we will learn about this God from studying this aspect of creation.

Of course, the devil is in the details. Exactly what it means to say that God "created by evolution" and then to work through the implications of that claim are wide open fields; not surprisingly, a lot of theologians have dived into this discussion headfirst.[8] My main point here, though, is that this question, "How does evolution help us understand something of who God is?," is a vital question to keep before us in our world today. It seems to me that familiar language of God, no matter how revered, is not adequate for the task before us.

Another Way

I hope no one thinks I invented the third option. I am, rather, thankful that over the years I have come into contact with Christian and Jewish thinkers who understand the powerful and inevitable role that science plays in our understanding of the natural world and therefore of the Creator of that world. And that understanding of the Creator, as

I said above, moves us to embrace the mystery of the Creator revealed to us by the mystery of the creation.

To pause for a second, that last paragraph is a good reminder of what I am after in this book: our experiences do in fact affect how we think about God. Those experiences can be personal, like literal blown elbows and moments of forced contemplation in a taxi. They also can be cosmic and global, rooted in the dawn of the universe and of life on this planet. What we have learned about the evolution of the cosmos, of the earth, and of living organisms is part of our collective experience in that it shapes our understanding of the nature of reality.

I am not suggesting that science explains everything. Neither am I saying science doesn't change over time. But science has uncovered some absolutely amazing things about our universe, namely that "evolution" is the key for understanding everything from galaxies to bacteria. As a matter of personal integrity, I need to embrace that we have something new to learn about the Creator as we have learned something new about the creation.

A huge and early step for me in moving forward has been to recognize what countless others have recognized before me—that the Bible is not suited to give answers to our scientific questions, nor does it need to be reconciled with science in order to remain religiously potent. The Bible does not speak the language of science, but of faith in God expressed in ancient ways, where creation happens in six days or a garden houses two enchanted trees and a talking serpent. Mining these stories for theological significance is good and right, but expecting them to somehow be agreeable to what we have learned through recently developed scientific methods using highly tuned technology is off the mark. It does no justice to science and, in my opinion, makes a mockery of Christian faith to boot.

Speaking of which, as far back as the fourth century, Augustine understood that Christians should steer clear of discussing cosmology by appealing to the Bible. He uses some strong words for those who would appeal to a literal reading of Genesis to explain how the cosmos came to be: "It is a disgraceful and dangerous thing for an infidel to hear a Christian, presumably giving the meaning of Holy Scripture, talking nonsense on these [cosmological] topics, and we should take all means to prevent such an embarrassing situation, in which people show up vast ignorance in a Christian and laugh it to scorn."[9]

In *The Great Partnership*, Rabbi Jonathan Sacks is at great pains to show that Judaism has historically made room for folding new scientific discoveries into its theology, even to the point of admitting when theology needs to be corrected by science. Sacks includes a fifteen-page appendix of quotations from various respected Jewish thinkers on several hot topics, including the importance of science for theology, reading the Bible nonliterally, the age of the universe, and evolution.

For example, the towering twelfth-century philosopher Maimonides considered the study of mathematics and physics to be necessary for attaining "human perfection" and insisted repeatedly that Genesis 1 should not be read literally. Instead, "God described these profound concepts [of creation], which His Divine wisdom found necessary to communicate to us, using allegories, metaphors, and imagery." In fact, like Augustine before him, Maimonides feared that reading Genesis literally "might lead us to conceive corrupt ideas and to form false opinions about God, or even entirely to abandon and reject"[10] faith itself. (Yay, Maimonides!)

Sacks also cites nineteenth-century rabbis who, following this train of thought, clearly felt evolution and Jewish tradition were not in conflict but in conversation. To his list I might add the names of two notably conservative Calvinist Christian theologians of the time, B. B. Warfield and Charles Hodge. I won't suggest that any of these thinkers would agree with me or anyone else living in the twenty-first century—a lot of water has passed under the bridge since their times—but the principle of conversation with rather than resistance to science is certainly there. In both Judaism and Christianity there is ample room not simply for doing science, but for *accepting the sacred responsibility to bring scientific knowledge into conversation with how we understand God.*

In the current climate such hopeful thoughts are too often drowned out by the revving engines of discord. Science and religion have been polarized for centuries, but not because there is an inevitable conflict between the two. The conflict arose because science collided not with Christianity, or even with the Bible, but with *literal* readings of Genesis. Many of us have heard of poor Galileo, who in the seventeenth century said the Earth revolved around the sun rather than being stationary (as the biblical authors assumed). He got into quite a lot of trouble for it (partly because he seems to have been something of a jerk). Eventually though, long after his death, the Catholic Church came around to his way of thinking. And the first probe sent to Jupiter was named after him.

Closer to our time and place is the famous "Scopes Monkey Trial" of 1925, where William Jennings Bryan and Clarence Darrow went toe-to-toe one hot week in Tennessee over whether science should be taught in public schools. More recently we had the rather unfortunate "intelligent design" legal case in 2005. After the Dover Area School Board in Pennsylvania required its high school teachers to "teach the controversy," that is, to teach intelligent design as a scientifically valid alternative to evolution, the court ruled that the board's move sought to pass off religious bias for scientific theory.

A distrust of science has gotten worse in recent years, especially with respect to the global pandemic and climate change. Opposition to science on religious grounds comes disproportionately from those who are not aware of the legacy of Judaism and Christianity and instead come from an option 1 mentality. But the choice between God or science is a false one. An option 3 mindset, which has a long and honored pedigree, believes that the world we live in has so much more to tell us about God than what we already know, because, as I've been saying, God is out ahead of us and always beyond our thoughts. In fact, God is *unimaginably* far out ahead of us, so unexpected, so steeped in mystery, so strange to our familiar thoughts, that we need creation to nudge us along. In that sense, science is a real aid in spiritual growth, not its enemy. Oh, the irony.

Evolution may be at odds with a *literal* reading of Genesis, but that does not make it at odds with God—or for that matter, with a reading of Genesis that respects its ancient setting.

A Better God Through Evolution

Genesis speaks of God as Creator of the cosmos and all of life, but it does so in ways that made sense to those who wrote those stories; they reflect ancient ways of thinking about how things came to be.

The authors were offering a portrait of their understanding of God based on their understanding of the physical world. Of course they were! With no reason to think otherwise, those authors believed that all the varieties of plants and animals, all mountains and valleys, all oceans and rivers are as God made them to be and remain fixed and permanent. Life did not evolve, mountains and earthquakes were not formed by shifts in tectonic plates, and rivers never cut their way through rocks. Everything was just "there." With respect to humans, the ancient Israelites knew exactly where babies come from, and reasoning backwards, they "knew" there was either one primordial, original couple to start the whole thing off (Adam and Eve) or a mass of couples as in Genesis 1.

We have known for more than 150 years that the biblical stories of creation breathed the same air as the stories from ancient Egypt, Mesopotamia, and Canaan. They tell us not so much what happened in history, but what ancient writers were saying about God or the gods. Comparing and contrasting these ancient stories has been a staple of biblical studies for generations, but without getting into all the ins and outs, we can sum it all up pretty quickly: Israel's creation stories mirrored the stories of their their cultural environment, but also distanced themselves from the common mindset of the day.

For example, the creation of a barrier overhead to keep the heavenly waters of chaos at bay is a feature shared by some of the ancient stories—in Genesis it is called *raqia* ("dome" or "vault," or in older translations, "firmament"). In Genesis, however, creation is a solo act by Israel's God and happens with no real exertion on God's part. God simply says, "Let there be . . ." and there it was. In other ancient stories, creation is a result of gods in bloody conflict over who is going to rule the roost. Another distinction concerns how God looks upon humans. In Genesis 1, all humans were created in God's "image and likeness" to rule over creation as God's second in command. In other ancient religions, such dignity is bestowed only on royalty.

And in Genesis 2, Adam is placed in the Garden of Eden to tend it in God's company, whereas other ancient stories portray humans as slaves to do the work that the gods do not want to deal with. Even in the story of Noah and the flood (Gen 6–9), which is a horrific story no matter how you slice it, humans are looked upon differently than they are in other ancient flood stories. In Genesis humans are wiped out because of their persistent inclination toward evil. In one Mesopotamian story, humans were drowned because they were making too much noise and disturbing the gods' rest.

Comparing these ancient stories is fascinating, both in how they are similar and in how they are different, but we can't spend time teasing all that out here, or this would turn into a very different kind of book. My point in going into any of this detail at all is to emphasize what we already glimpsed in Chapter 6 with the hymn to Aten: the ancient Israelites understood their God within the "science" of the day, in conversation with the way other nations portrayed the cosmos and their gods' role in creating it. Yes, the Israelites drew some thick lines between the role their God played compared with the role the other gods played, but everyone was working with a broadly accepted picture of physical reality. And that picture was not the picture we see according to modern science. We should not expect it to be.

How we talk about the God of creation today must also work with the broadly accepted scientific picture of our physical reality. It seems to me that this means embracing a thought that never had to be (and could not have been) uttered throughout most of the history of Christianity and Judaism: *evolution is God's way of creating.*

But what does *that* mean? Good question, but we don't need to arrive at quick answers. Theology's wheels turn slowly, and we don't need to have the answers first before we can get on with life. Working out challenging issues in real time is *part of the life of faith*, not a prelude to the life of faith. I should add, however, that when I say evolution is God's way of creating, I don't mean to suggest that God intervenes from the outside and directs evolution like a conductor of an orchestra. I mean that God "inhabits" the process of evolution, not micromanaging it, but by being the divine Presence that lives in every particle of it. I am not sure how that last sentence will strike you, though we will come back to this idea in a later chapter and I hope it might make a little more sense then. But I am simply trying to give some language to God that renders justice to what we know to be true about our universe. That is the science of our day, so that is what we need to work with.

One vital implication of God creating through evolution is the sacredness of all life: the Creator sees all living things as endowed with divine worth, including the grass in the fields, the birds in the air, the Dole banana on my kitchen counter—and even my yeast-like students who fail open-book tests. Even though humans have unique capacities compared with any other species on the planet—like abstract thought where we "think about thinking" and are "conscious about consciousness"—all living things have DNA. All of life is interconnected, and no one part, I believe, is valued as less sacred by the Creator.

The interconnectedness of all of life gives me a sound Christian grounding for speaking against unholy exploitation of any living thing for our greed. Not only should no human be trafficked, but no animal should suffer before it is consumed (and some will say they should not be consumed at all). Ecosystems should not be leveled for corporate greed but protected by us as those complex organisms who share the land. All of creation is sacred, which is also central to indigenous religions that flourished before European exploitation of the land. As *Yellowstone*'s John Dutton (Kevin Costner) observed, the problem before us is that "people stopped livin' with the land and started livin' on it."[11]

As much as evolution wreaks havoc with a literal reading of the creation stories in Genesis, to those so inclined, it helps expand our minds to understand God differently. Creation is shouting to us something of the deep mystery of the character of God and of creation. Pitting evolution *against* the Bible, or Christianity, or God is a missed opportunity to make God relatable to ourselves and to others.

I'd like to drop a quick hint here of something we glimpsed earlier and will see again later on. Evolution drives us to think differently about God because evolution is ongoing—God's creative work did not end at the dawn of time. Some theologians add that an evolutionary cosmos implies a purpose to the universe—evolution is heading toward a goal. That idea appeals to me, and if we are going to bring God and evolution together, it seems to me that purpose has to be on the table.

When we begin talking like this, we have certainly left the realm of biblical literalism, which deals with none of these things. The creation as we understand it today is telling us something about God that the Bible doesn't. But rather than seeing evolution as the enemy of faith that must be squashed, I see it as a curveball that drives me to adjust what I think I know of God. And the God whom I see when I ponder the nature of life on this earth brings me to a humbling awareness that I am a part of a big interconnected whole, where God's creative Presence and energy infuse all living things.

The Bigger Picture

Human evolution has been the focus of controversy among many Christians for generations, but it is only one small part of a larger picture. As I've been saying, evolution is not simply about where people come from, or even how life as a whole came to be on our planet. *Evolution is the sweeping, all-inclusive scientific landscape of constant change by which we explain the cosmos and what it contains.*[12] It is the big story within which we understand our physical reality. As theologian Ilia Delio puts it, "In my view, evolution *is* the story, the meta-narrative of our age. It is not only a scientific explanation for physical reality; it is, rather, the overarching description of reality, the cosmological framework for all contemporary thought." It will not do to isolate human evolution and "deal with it." Human evolution is one part of a larger picture of *changing* reality that helps give us an expanded vision of our understanding of God.

Our home planet did not pop into existence fully formed, but emerged—evolved, as it were—from gases and grains of dust orbiting the fledgling sun that were pulled together by gravity over many millions of years to form a sphere. Thus began its 4.5-billion-year transformation from an inhospitable furnace to a world of water and oxygen, magnetic poles that protect us from solar wind, ozone that shields us from ultraviolet rays, and hundreds of other tweaks and adjustments to make our world a home where evolution could yield an explosion of countless species of vegetation and animal life.

Likewise, the cosmos as a whole was not always as it is now but has been evolving for about fourteen billion years since the Big Bang, which many cosmologists think is a plausible theory of the origins of the universe.[13] According to that theory, everything that exists was once condensed in one very small point called the "singularity," which then exploded its energy out into the void. After about ten thousand years that energy began coalescing into matter.

Yay matter! Matter is huge because it makes up everything we can see or touch, including us. Very large objects in the matter category are stars, which began forming when the universe was somewhere between 100,000 and 250,000 years old.[14]

We really can't say enough about stars. Before they came along, hydrogen and helium, with a little lithium, beryllium, and boron[15] (elements 1–5 on the periodic table of the elements that we've all forgotten), were the only elements in the universe. Those are great elements, don't get me wrong. Hydrogen is a big part of water, and helium, when inhaled, can make you a huge hit at kids' parties. But they don't help us very much with respect to being alive. Where are nitrogen, oxygen, sodium, magnesium, potassium, calcium, and iron, to name just a few? They were formed when the first five elements came together to form stars. For reasons I don't understand (apart from what I picked up from Homer Simpson's line of work), stars create thermonuclear fusion reactions, which lead to the creation of those other heavier elements I just listed (and others).

Of course, vital elements tucked away in stars do us no good. Those stars need to explode, which is what they do when they get old and become supernovas and blast those elements out into the universe. As the theory goes, like dandelion seeds in the wind, the elements from some of those explosions hitched a ride on cold rocks and, as in our case, found their way to our planet where they encountered the right conditions for life. And along the way, stars came together under the pull of gravity—hundreds of billions of them—to form galaxies, and those galaxies formed galaxy clusters that span the cosmos.

The point of this possibly traumatic stroll through memories of high school science classes is simply to remind us of a bit of common knowledge: the universe did not appear as it is now. It began very small and literally blew up and is still expanding, growing, changing, developing. Like the Earth and life on it, the universe emerged a long time ago and continues to blossom. For those of us who believe that a Creator is responsible for all there is, that Creator seems to be in the habit of creating not once and done, not in fixed permanence, but by constant emergence.

This creates in me a sense of jaw-dropping, deer-in-the-headlights awe, where words are out of place. A changing, unfolding universe does not rob God of glory. It declares it—though finding that space takes major adjustments in my thinking about God. Perhaps it has for you as well.

Chapter 8

Other People (Eww. I Mean, Yay.)

I LEFT GRADUATE SCHOOL at age thirty-three and was a seminary professor for the next fourteen years . . . until I wasn't. I touched on this episode a bit earlier, and a slightly fuller version can be found in *The Bible Tells Me So* and *The Sin of Certainty*, for those of you who just have to be all up in my business. Long story short, for the next four years I cobbled together a living by writing, speaking, adjunct teaching, and another venture or two in a limping attempt to mimic positive cash flow. Actually, I was in limbo for only three-and-a-half years, but in order to forge meaning out of a tough situation, I've always said "four" to play off of the biblical idea of desert wandering, be it Israel's forty years or Jesus's forty days.

Money was very tight and my anxiety spiked, but working out of my hundred-and-fifty-square-foot basement office with no windows and a periodic water seepage problem introduced me to a new challenge: enforced loneliness. I'm an introvert, so I'm just fine, thank you very much, being alone on a daily basis, but this was too much even for me. By comparison, COVID isolation posed no challenge to me whatsoever—perhaps the years of my basement trial helped me gird up my loins, to use the biblical expression.

That being said, being alone with your thoughts for a few years with no one to bounce them off of except pets and your laptop screen is not something I'd recommend. I did get a lot done, which made my Germanic checklist mentality very happy, but I also went slightly bonkers. I realized that . . . hmm . . . I need people. Occasional adjunct teaching gigs or academic conferences weren't enough.

Thankfully, I received an email one day from the provost at a nearby Christian university. Apparently without bothering to run any background checks, they offered me a position in the undergraduate Bible department. Let's just say I was very happy, not just because this school was a great fit for me, and not just because positive cash flow would now become a hittable mark, but because . . . people. I missed the camaraderie with colleagues and students. Now once again I had a chance to be grounded in a community of faith, support, mutual respect, acceptance, and dare I say love.

The most unexpected lesson I would learn during my wilderness period was the rather alarming idea that engagement with other people actually shapes how I think about God. Actually, more than that: a central way *that* I experience God is through other people. But what made this experience a curveball for me was not this simple realization, which, when it works well, is a beautiful thing. Rather, it was the capacity that people of faith can have for treating each other horribly and how *that* shapes our view of God, too. How we experience God is determined in no small measure by how we experience each other.

The primary value of the above-mentioned tradition I was a part of for many years was its claim to hold to orthodox beliefs about God. And since orthodoxy was the primary value of that community, treating others harshly for failing to be orthodox was not only tolerated but valued because doing so was in the service of protecting orthodoxy. During those years, I would come to see some friends leave that community and others leave the faith entirely; what kick-started that process was the community's harsh, unyielding, unmerciful, unjust treatment of them. As for myself, after I left, it did not take long for me to experience a great distance from God, to the point that I seriously doubted God's existence for some time.

I've been talking a lot about how my experiences of blown elbows, taxi rides, graduate school, galaxies, and evolution have led (pushed) me to understand God differently—especially to see faith as an embrace of the mystery of God. But it took my time in isolation from any community to help bring this thought more down to earth. For better or for worse, I came to see how experience of others is tied to our experience of God.

A spiritual community that exists largely to shelter its members from outsiders, or that sees "fellowship" as exchanging brief niceties during the service and Sunday school, is not a spiritual community. What binds a spiritual community together isn't (or at least shouldn't be) homogeny of race, ethnicity, economic status, or geography. It's not even the beliefs and traditions that distinguish that community from others—and it is certainly not the personal fallout of the knock-down-drag-out fights that happen over orthodoxy. As I see it, what binds a spiritual community together is love, because God is love, and love in community is how we experience God in our day-to-day lives. And what can tear a community apart quicker than debates about this or that belief is treating each other horribly.

No One Has Ever Seen God

The Bible is not big on the idea of people being able to see God. On Mount Sinai, Moses did catch a glimpse of God's back, but that is more a weird exception. In fact, "seeing" God that way is not actually seeing God at all, unless you think the God of the infinite cosmos has a body like ours. At least some ancient Israelites seemed to have harbored such thinking, but I confess I do not. The New Testament is likewise on board with not seeing God. Yes, we see Jesus—actually, *they* did, *we* don't. But even for Jesus's contemporaries, God was "up there" in the heavens and Jesus was down here pointing the way. As a rule, God might be sometimes heard or else perceived by the Spirit, but not seen. I think we can all relate. People today don't see God either, and if they say they have, we don't believe them.

The author of the first letter of John is quite adamant about this. In chapter 4, verse 12, we read, "No one has ever seen God." Truer words were never spoken, but, I have to admit, it would sure help if we did. People say that seeing God would supposedly blow away our senses or some such terrible outcome. Fine, but how about an indirect sighting, as in the good old days—a voice from a burning bush or frightening whirlwind? How hard can it be? If I can't see God with one or more of my five senses, I just want some sign so I can know God is there. Judging from many conversations, I am not alone.

What makes matters worse is that what we actually *can* see and *do* know doesn't exactly help. I have a number of atheist/agnostic friends in my life who don't believe in God precisely because they see no evidence for God. Acts of God that people used to point to—like the weather or locust plagues—are now explained as natural occurrences that obey natural laws. Whereas I see the universe telling me surprising new things about God, they see the lack of evidence as proof there is no God at all. I get it. We are used to verifying things by evidence.

Even though we are separated by two millennia, I do think we share something with John's community. I mean, why does John bother to bring up "No one has ever seen God"? Conventional scholarly wisdom says that sixty or more years had passed since the time of Jesus, which means two or more generations of people had been born who never saw Jesus for themselves and only heard of him from stories old-timers told—no evidence. I can well imagine people becoming uninterested in a movement so out of touch with its founder. Another similar ancient movement, the Essene community that gave us the Dead Sea Scrolls, likewise had a charismatic leader, but that movement couldn't weather more than one generation or two after his death. It is not hard to imagine the same concern rising up in John's community.

As we'll see in a moment, John seems intent on including these latecomers into the mystery of God. We glimpsed this in Chapter 6 in the story of Doubting Thomas. After Jesus rose from the dead, he appeared to the disciples and breathed on them the Holy Spirit, but Thomas for some reason wasn't there. When he showed up and the other disciples told him what happened, Thomas wasn't buying it: "Unless I see the mark of the nails in his hands, and put my finger in the mark of the nails and my hand in his side, I will not believe" (John 20:25). A week later, Jesus returned and, as if to make a point, just appeared in a locked room and headed right to Thomas, telling him to touch the wounds in his hands and on his side, which he did. Now Thomas believed, and Jesus responded, "Have you believed because you have seen me? Blessed are those who have not seen and yet have come to believe" (John 20:29).

I dare say that we are in a similar boat as the readers of John's Gospel and letters.[1] We have no firsthand physical acquaintance with Jesus of Nazareth, let alone God. "Where is God and how do we know?" are active questions for many of us, including me.

John's solution to this problem in the verses that follow is one that has challenged my understanding of God and the nature of faith. Though God cannot be seen, John's first letter doesn't leave it at that. The entire verse reads: "No one has ever seen God; if we love one another, God lives in us, and his love is perfected in us" (1 John 4:12). To get the full force of this, replace the semicolon with "but" or "however," because that's what the author means: *No one has ever seen God, but if we love one another, God lives in us . . .*

This is certainly another mystery passage. God is love, and so we "see" God by mimicking God's love; though we cannot physically see God, we can experience God through the love of others.

This idea is one of those things about the Christian faith that stretches my brain and makes me want to reevaluate my priorities. "Evidence" of God is not gained with a bigger telescope, higher math, or more clever argument. God is experienced in mutually vulnerable relationality—which is just a fancy way of describing how God in Christ loves the world. If I want to experience God's loving Presence, I am to love others by mimicking God's love for me. Living this way is risky. It involves laying aside my ego, becoming vulnerable, and putting others first, regardless of how I think they might respond to me.

One might be tempted to say, "That's it? That's all I have to do?! Just love and I see God?!" As if love is easy. Speaking from personal experience, loving others first is hard work—it would seem contrary to our natures. Seeing God in the messy humanity of others and not despite it has been for me a radically challenging notion about God. It makes it all so . . . earthy and messy.

I imagine, too, that it may feel like a divine cop-out to put all the burden on us for how or whether people experience or don't experience God. It really depends on us?! But what if it does? And what if that isn't an afterthought or "the best God can do under the circumstances"? What if that's how God works in the world? What if we "are" God to each other—not literally, but what if God is actually Present in the cosmos *through us*? To put that in Christian terms, what if we are Jesus to each other, in whom God dwells and through whom we see God? Again, not literally "Jesus," but what if God's Presence in Christ is in some sense also true of us all?

At any rate, in the biblical tradition, God seems to have quite a connection with humanity. And in the Christian story, God is enfleshed as a first-century working-class Jewish male named Jesus. John's opening of his Gospel, "the Word became flesh and lived among us," should alert us that working through flesh is how God seems to act—not as an "up there" deity who makes cameo appearances, but one who works through humanity, Jesus in particular, and then in me and the rest of us.

I can't help but think that the pressure's on for how we are to act, but experiencing God (who *is* love) through the love of the community is actually what we would expect from an enfleshing God of love.

I'm not saying I fully grasp this, or see the logic—after all, remember that Jesus's incarnation, which ties all this together, is itself a profound and incomprehensible mystery. But once we put some pieces together, the idea that the infinite God of the cosmos indwells all flesh, indeed, all creation, sounds quite normal, if also difficult to comprehend. We'll come back to this in Chapter 10.

Unfortunately, as I mentioned, all this sounds great until it doesn't. All sorts of things can go wrong with this plan. If how people love can show us God to one another, then not loving can rip God away quicker than any argument.

A Partial Theory About Why Christians Can Be Horrible Humans

Over the years I have been struck, surprised even, by how many people have left not only their communities of faith but any faith at all because of how they were treated by other Christians. Why doesn't loving one another with the love of God, who is love, get the traction is deserves? I have a theory. And let me say that I have been on both sides of the equation, which makes me something of an expert.

Many have experienced animosity in Christian contexts, and—at least in my little universe—particularly in evangelical and fundamentalist contexts. No, not everyone in these movements is guilty. Just give me a second to explain, please.

These two movements are not identical. In fact, evangelicalism arose in the middle of the twentieth century as a reaction to fundamentalism, with its highly literalistic view of the Bible, selective rejection of science, and general isolation from anything deemed "worldly." Nowadays, however, at least in popular culture, it is hard to distinguish the two, and they are typically collapsed together simply as "evangelicalism"—a historical faux pas that is here to stay, much to the consternation of some evangelicals I know who try very hard to maintain the distinction, though I think that horse has left the barn.

All that being said, as distinct as these groups may be in certain important respects, they share a core feature: both are *deeply intellectual movements.*

To any who have left these movements, or to those on the outside looking in with bewilderment, this claim may sound odd. "Exvangelicals" and others have left the faith of their youth in part because they got weary of the deafening intellectual echo chamber and mental alchemy it took for them to stay. All that may be true, but evangelicalism and fundamentalism are nonetheless intellectual movements. Why? Because their core values are *doctrines*—a collection of *beliefs* about God, Jesus, the nature and ultimate fate of humanity, and biblical inerrancy (the Bible is always right on whatever topic it deliberately addresses), among other matters.

Doctrines are carefully worked out ideas—*thoughts*—the products of centuries-long, word-smithed battles against other ideas and that are deemed essential to faith, nonnegotiable, binding, and absolutely valid for all who want to claim the Christian faith as their own. And because these doctrines are so vital, an extensive and well-rehearsed apologetics industry exists to protect their *intellectual* credibility. Believing the right things is seen as a core value of faith. In my opinion, it is considered to be *the* core value of faith.

Now, before any of you have an aneurism, I do believe there are such things as doctrines in Christianity—faith has content. Sets of beliefs are important for giving various communities of faith parameters for how they believe. In fact, defining core beliefs is fully unavoidable whenever people gather together for a common purpose, religious or otherwise. But when strict adherence to ideas, sometimes a rather extensive list of them, is driving the car, other things—such as love, vulnerability, and humility[2]—are either moved to the back seat or tossed in the truck, if not out the window entirely.

It is no secret that animosities, even violent ones, have arisen in the history of Christianity over who has the best ideas. Years ago, I brought this up to a seminary student of mine, who did not see such belligerence as the unfortunate cost of doing holy business, but as a core value: smiting your enemy is a holy Christian personality trait. I asked him, "Where does love fit in?" I remember the stunned look on his face, as if I were suddenly speaking Coptic. "Love?!" he said. "That's just what liberals say to avoid pure doctrine." I don't remember the details of what transpired, but I can tell you neither of us left the conversation convinced of the other's point of view.

Love is an easy casualty when maintaining that ideas are the core value, and especially when maintaining them is tied to the reality of God's existence. In addition, our lived experiences, the topic of this book, make no dent whatsoever in strongly held doctrine. Surely (as I've heard many times), the permanent, biblically based God-ordained doctrines do not change on the whim of taking taxi rides and peering at distant galaxies. In fact, our experiences are utterly untrustworthy and to be held in deep suspicion, because they are tainted by original sin and are therefore fertile ground for Satan to sow seeds of unbelief. Experiences must be brought into line with church doctrine, not the other way around.

I do understand the logic. Any intellectualized system of beliefs about God *must* minimize "subjective" things like love and experience in favor of right ideas. The problem, though—and I feel this is almost too obvious to say—is that (1) "right ideas" are not downloaded from heaven but created throughout history in the context of subjective human experience, and (2) Christian faith (not to mention Judaism) from its very biblical beginning has always been highly relational and experiential, involving our whole being, not just the maintenance of a lengthy list of beliefs.

There are more productive ways in the history of Christianity to think about "right thinking." You may be familiar with the Wesleyan Quadrilateral. It sounds like a dance move, and in a way it is. According to the founder of the Methodist movement, John Wesley (1703–1791), the Quadrilateral is a way of explaining how we arrive at our beliefs about God. These four things—scripture, tradition, reason, and experience—work together. *Scripture* is the primary source for what Christians believe, but how we understand scripture and what we take from it are unavoidably affected by the other three factors: the particular flavor of Christian *tradition* that formed us, our ability to *reason* through what we are reading, and our manifold *experiences* as encultured human beings. Faith reflects our full humanity, and not humanity as an abstract quality, but our fully enfleshed humanity: the Quadrilateral dance is not the same for every time and place.

A similar scheme is the Episcopal three-legged stool, attributed to Church of England theologian Richard Hooker (1554–1600): scripture, tradition, and reason work together to help put our faith into words. This three-legged stool leaves off experience as a potential fourth leg, but that's fine. Experience isn't ignored. It's actually basic to the other three—engaging *scripture*, employing *reason*, and living out of our *tradition* are, technically speaking, all human experiences. I wouldn't blame you if you felt this was too fine a distinction, and ignore it if it doesn't help, but the Episcopal scheme rings true to me.

The point, however, is the same, regardless: the life of faith is not essentially an objective intellectual quest for establishing abstract beliefs, where the rest of our humanity hangs in the background. Faith is not merely repeating what the "Bible says," nor what our church traditions tell us, and nor is it simply bending unreflectively to a given experience. Being human means all three (or four) factors are inextricably tied together.

Our God-talk is invariably tied to our humanity. This means to me that we should be open to conversing in love with anybody about anything, even those ideas that we see as central and nonnegotiable.

Roman Catholic mystic Richard Rohr has taken this scheme a step further. For him, how we understand God is analogous to a tricycle[3]— its three wheels are experience, scripture, and tradition. I like how experience is mentioned specifically, and Rohr (rightly, I think) includes reason as a dimension of human experience. But the real breakthrough of this analogy for me is that experience is the front wheel that guides the back wheels of scripture and tradition. In fact, Rohr insists that we all do this anyway, even when we think we are simply reading the Bible "plainly."

By placing experience at the front, Rohr is not minimizing the role of the sacred text in the life of faith. He is simply acknowledging how our varied human experiences are what make us human and shape how we see *absolutely everything*, including scripture. The tricycle absolutely needs all three wheels, but our experience is primary for what direction our God-talk takes. The other great distinction between the tricycle and the stool or Quadrilateral, particularly given the theme of this book, is that the tricycle *moves*—it is a dynamic rather than a static system.

I truly understand how all this might sound problematic to some, but the central role of experience in the life of faith is widely recognized now in academic circles as a no-brainer. For the past few hundred years in the Western world, it has typically been thought that theology and the study of the Bible were more or less objective, "scientific" undertakings. That idea began to take a big hit in the latter half of the twentieth century, when people started noticing that . . . uh . . . well, there is really no such thing as being truly objective about *anything*, and certainly not about how we read the Bible or understand God. The modern academic study of the Bible and theology, with its methods and the questions it deems are even worth asking, is the product of white, affluent, Western-educated, straight, Eurocentric males.

We have a saying at *The Bible for Normal People* podcast that tries to capture this reality: "All theology has an adjective." No approach can claim to be unaffected by the experiences that make us human. There is no pure "theology" to be contrasted to "*feminist* theology" or "*Black* theology," because the supposed pure theology is driven by its own encultured concerns and assumptions.

I believe that no human tribe can capture the divine. We are staring into mystery—a mystery that can be experienced, even as we see only "in part" or "dimly," to borrow Paul's words. And so, we need each other, bound together in the love of God, where all those of goodwill, mercy, and humility have a seat at the table, and no one tradition gets to hold court as the final divine authority. Here, too, we are seeing an enfleshing God at work: God speaks not only through creation but through us all.

Something Happened

Some of you may remember the 2013 story of Ohio Republican senator Rob Portman, a Methodist who reversed his position on gay marriage two years after his son come came out to him. In a newspaper opinion piece, he wrote:

> *I have come to believe* that if two people are prepared to make a lifetime commitment to love and care for each other in good times and in bad, the government shouldn't deny them the opportunity to get married.
>
> *That isn't how I've always felt.* As a Congressman, and more recently as a Senator, I opposed marriage for same-sex couples. Then, *something happened* that led me to think through my position in a much deeper way. (My emphasis.)[4]

Portman changed his mind because "something happened." I imagine Portman's son caught a glimpse of God's love in his father's love. And as for Portman, his love for his son led not simply to changing his views on gay marriage. The deeper change was how he saw God—a God who two years earlier was "clearly" opposed to same-sex unions was now accepting of them. Portman's experience led to a change in how he understood God—which is a nice summary of what this book is about.

When we show love to one another, a lot changes. I have found, like Senator Portman, that seeing the love of God in others does not just happen with people we agree with. It may happen with people who hold views we find odious. In the parable of the Good Samaritan in Luke's Gospel, the one whose love of neighbor truly reflects the

face of God is a Samaritan, whom many Jews at the time saw as religious pretenders, practitioners of a false version of Judaism, and to be
shunned. In my own life, I have been surprised so often by who reflects
the love of God to me that I've stopped being surprised.

One moment in particular keeps coming back to me, though I was
only an observer. When one of my teenaged children was in recovery
from anxiety and depression, she was very self-critical and felt that her
continued struggles were due to some defect that made her unworthy
of love, especially her own. Her mentor, a therapist in his fifties and
not himself Christian (at least not as far as I could tell), stopped her
short and asked, "You believe in God, right? Don't you know that you
are of unconditional worth?"

That was an expression of love that let my daughter see God differently. It also almost instantly cleared away a lot of the perfectionistic
"God-is-disappointed-in-you-if-you-have-bad-doctrine" internal rhet-
oric that had enmeshed itself in my own heart and soul, and instead to
see God as . . . someone who is not out to get me. (What a crazy idea.
Who'd have thought?)

And then another thought entered my mind that day some fifteen
years ago: *I'm forty-seven years old. Why am I hearing this now for the
first time? In fact, why have I never heard this in a sermon or anywhere in
church and instead was fed a diet of why we are right, the people out there
are wrong, and let's make sure we keep it that way?* That thought didn't
make me angry. It made me sad at how much time we had wasted not
being aware that we are surrounded by and infused with the love of a
God who *is* love. That doesn't mean "happy times forever." It means
all of us, as we are, are loved by God, and we are on a journey of faith
that will include both very hard times, perhaps unbearably so, and also
times of joy as we try daily, with God's Spirit in us, to live into that
reality. And I mourn that I did not internalize that thought earlier,
before my wife and I had children.

• • •

To see God in the love of another is not restricted to one religion or to any religion at all, let alone one version of a religion. As happened to my daughter with her therapist, I have often been moved to experience God and adjust my understanding of God because of the love shown to me by those far removed from my familiar spiritual surroundings.

It seems that the glory of God is not just shouting at us from the edges of the cosmos, or from the beauty of the diverse life on our planet, but from those glimpses of God's love we see in each other, our neighbors, whoever might cross our path. I try to internalize those glimpses and carry them with me each day.

Chapter 9

Quantum Weirdness

Y OU HAVE TO BE really smart to understand math-driven sciences. I'm not. I'm smart in other ways, like: I'm the only person in my family who knows how exactly to position the pee pad to make sure the dog hits it. I am also the only person in my extended family who understands how to load a dishwasher properly, meaning knowing which items can be slightly overlapped and by how much without stressing the system. If you think that's easy or unimportant, then you're part of the problem. I have other such talents I'd love to tell you about, but, to return to my point, science isn't among them.

Which is too bad. As a boy, I *really* wanted to be an astronomer, but math and I stopped getting along somewhere around algebra in seventh grade. Still, I tried gutting out an astronomy major my first semester of college, but that dream ended by October. An earlier dream also went by the wayside. As a young child, like most red-blooded American boys born in the 1960s, I first wanted to be an astronaut. I am not exactly sure what happened in my young life that led me to abandon this gallant quest, but it might have had something to do with not wanting to go someplace where there is no air and the only things keeping me from dying a gruesome death were a few clips and latches on my spacesuit and a very thin space capsule that you just had to trust had an absolutely zero chance of leaking.

Crushed dreams notwithstanding, I continue to be drawn to science and the lure of catching a glimpse of big and marvelous things. And for that, thankfully, you don't have to be a trained expert to hang in there. I can grasp the basic ideas of evolution, like genetic mutations or natural selection, without needing to fully understand the ins and outs of how those things happen on a biochemical level. And though the universe is unfathomably large and old, size and age are concepts I can grasp. But with quantum physics, all hope for me of grasping anything flies out the window.

Quantum physics has been a curveball for me, because it presents a universe of the infinitely small that challenges our notions of reality. I will never understand, in any meaningful sense of the word "understand," what quantum physicists talk about, other than the fact that I feel helpless when I try to—like my ankle is caught in the rigging of a weather balloon as it takes off and climbs into the stratosphere. And with a universe this weird and chaotic, what do I do with God who made it all and whom I want to claim to "know"?

And yet, it is precisely the unsettling weirdness of the quantum world that has opened up for me fresh ways of understanding God. Had I not been willing to face squarely the quantum curveball, I would not have seen how some familiar ideas about God and Jesus can take on an unexpected and life-giving depth and richness.

But let's leave God and Jesus for the next chapter. Let's talk first about the curveball of quantum weirdness.

Not to Worry. We're All Dumb.

Quantum physics is the branch of physics, just over a hundred years old, that deals with how things work on the atomic and subatomic levels of reality. "Quantum" (Latin "how much") refers to the fact that all matter and energy can be broken down into discreet unimaginably small units, sometimes referred to as packets. And I mean *small*. Protons and neutrons, which make up an atom's nucleus, are about 10^{-15} meters in diameter, a ridiculously small number.[1] If you wanted to get down to that level, you would need to slice up a meter stick into one billion segments and then take one of those segments and slice it up a million times more. *That's* a proton.

And protons are not the smallest things out there. As unimaginably large as the numbers were when we talked about the universe, they are that unimaginably small at the quantum level. And, if it helps to ponder it all, we humans, according to some measurements, are size-wise roughly at the midway point of all physical objects in the universe.[2]

As it turns out, once we peer deep down into the scale of the very small, the universe behaves in ways for which we, who live in the world of the very large things, have no frame of reference. As far as we are concerned, an ice cube cannot also be a pool of liquid, nor can one twin's eating a bad burrito give the other twin an upset stomach thousands of miles away. These two *very* inadequate analogies might at least give a hint of what quantum physics reveals to us about the universe of the very small. Things do get weird, and when physicists start talking about multiple universes because it "makes sense" mathematically, I know I'm just going along for a ride.

By contrast, the laws of motion and gravity that Sir Isaac Newton so kindly worked out for us three hundred years ago are more or less within our frame of reference. For example, every object has a precisely defined position and velocity. I am sitting at my desk right now, which is my position, and my velocity is zero (even though I fidget). And some of Newton's equations, though genius, are not so abstract as to make no sense to nonscientific big-world dwellers like myself, such as Force = Mass × Acceleration ($F = ma$). I get it. I went to high school. A car that weighs one thousand pounds traveling at thirty miles per hour will hit a cement wall with less force than a tractor-trailer at sixty miles per hour. A toddler running at me will not knock me over. An NFL linebacker will knock me into next week.

Newton revolutionized our understanding of the universe, but at the end of the day his insights are not literally universal. They work perfectly well for us humans on the large, day-in-and-day-out level, and also on the astronomical scale, but they don't work at all on the quantum level. To explain quantum reality, a new physics and a new kind of math (beyond the calculus that Newton invented) were needed. And with that, what we mean by "reality" has been in a state of debate for a century.

As unruly as it is, quantum physics is not smoke and mirrors. It is science and has had remarkable success on a practical level. We have all benefited from quantum theory. GPSs, MRIs, LEDs, transistors, electron microscopes, not to mention atomic clocks, supercomputers, uncrackable codes, and lasers are examples of quantum physics at work to make our lives more efficient and comfy. On a theoretical level, however, quantum physicists themselves are quick to admit, "Yeah, we still don't *really* know what's going on here. We just know the math checks out." After one hundred years physicists have still not been able to arrive at a solid, agreed-upon model to explain how and why the quantum world does what it does.

For us mortals, the ignorance is compounded by the fact that the following "basic" equation of quantum physics looks like my cat peed on my keyboard and broke it:

$$i\hbar \frac{\partial}{\partial t} \psi(\mathbf{r},t) = -\frac{\hbar^2}{2m} \nabla^2 \psi(\mathbf{r},t) + V(\mathbf{r},t)\psi(\mathbf{r},t)$$

I think I copied that correctly, but if not, you'll never know, which is my point. The "Schrödinger equation" describes the quantum world in terms of wave behavior.[3] Yes, it's a heady piece of information I don't claim to understand, and backed up by some heady math I absolutely do not understand. But the Schrödinger equation is about as fundamental to quantum physicists as the times table is to the rest of us. But even with high-powered math, the strange world of subatomic particles continues to puzzle the elite minds on the planet.

So, naturally, I—the guy who was crushed by junior high school algebra—feel ready to take it on.

I'm not at all ready, but I want to try anyway, because what I've come to understand about quantum physics has challenged me—as have evolution and cosmology—to adjust how I think about the nature of creation and therefore to adjust how I think about the nature of the Creator, not to mention the nature of my own existence. You should also know, if you don't already, that quantum physicists don't all agree with each other. Some of the in-house tiffs are legendary and downright catty.[4] Different interpretations of quantum reality abound, but by any interpretation, quantum physics has stretched my imagination and taken me a bit further into the deep, fascinating, intriguing mystery of the universe and the God I believe created it.

Even the physics of the very small will affect how I think about God, if in fact I believe that God is the God of quantum reality as much as of Newton's universe.

Reality That Bends

Diving into quantum physics means first taking a brief look at the most famous scientist ever. You know who.

My favorite two photos of Albert Einstein are the one where he is sticking out his (remarkably long) tongue and the other where he is riding a bicycle, I suppose in vain attempts to convince people he was seminormal. The fact is that Einstein was not normal. Not by a long shot. He couldn't really be bothered to jump through academic hoops, and when he couldn't land a decent teaching job like the rest of his doctoral classmates, he took a tedious nine-to-five job as a Swiss patent clerk. And in spare moments, left alone with his thoughts, he shifted the entire history of physics and transformed our understanding of reality bequeathed to us by Newton.

Einstein's presence loomed large for decades, and still does nearly seventy years after his death. What put him on the map is something nearly everyone has heard of: the theory of relativity. Actually, there were two such theories, the special theory and the general theory, but I'm not trying to write a science textbook and my brain is already tired, so let's keep this simple for both our sakes.

It turns out that some things that humans have always taken for granted as constant and stable in the universe are actually not, such as . . . oh, I don't know . . . TIME!![5] Einstein demonstrated that time is not what we think it is—it does not pass at a constant rate for everyone.

For all practical purposes, a second is a second, a minute is a minute, etc. Every smart watch on Earth is synchronized to the same exact present moment (apart from time zones). But that is only our limited perception. The truth is stranger. Time actually passes more slowly the closer one is to a massive object (like Earth) and more quickly the farther one is away from that object. This means that time passes more slowly for those living at sea level than those living in a high rise—though I suppose I can gain some solace from the fact that Biff and Buffy living in their 136th-floor, sixty-six-million-dollar, seven-thousand-square-foot Central Park Tower penthouse condo will age more quickly than the doorman who has to be polite to them. Though we shouldn't gloat. Technically, our head ages faster than our feet.[6]

Einstein showed as well that speed also affects the perceived passage of time. Someone moving quickly past the Earth's surface will experience time move more slowly compared with those stationary on Earth. Astronauts orbiting the earth in a space station and vacationers flying to Hawaii age more slowly than those who are earthbound.

This might be a little confusing, since not two paragraphs ago I said that Biff and Buffy will age more quickly than the doorman because they are farther from the Earth's mass. That is true and is called "gravitational time dilation." But "relative velocity time dilation" is also a thing: speed slows down time, too. The reason why astronauts on the International Space Station age more *slowly* than people on Earth, even though they are farther from the Earth's mass, is that they are zipping around the Earth at five miles per second.[7] That speed factor has a greater effect of slowing down time than does their distance factor from the Earth in speeding up their time.

Got it? Not really? Me neither. Let's move on.

These sorts of time differences can be perceived only by atomic measurement devices, which they have been. The differences would be experienced more dramatically if a traveler were near a massive black hole, which has so much mass that even light cannot escape, or when nearing the speed of light. On the latter point, for example, a round trip to Alpha Centauri (4.25 light-years each way), traveling at 80 percent the speed of light, would take about ten years from our Earthbound perspective. The astronauts, however, would age only about six years, because—say it with me—speed slows down time.[8] Jodie Foster's dropping capsule experience in *Contact* and Matthew McConaughey's library scene in *Interstellar* try to depict the fluidity of time that results from the effects of relativity.

The relativity of time is too profound a thought to be skimmed over. In fact, the popular physicist Carlo Rovelli reminds us that at least some physicists and philosophers "have come to the conclusion that the idea of a present that is common to the whole universe is an illusion and that the 'flow' of time is a generalization that doesn't work."[9] A generalization? How we perceive literally everything is a generalization?! Not all physicists see the flow of time as an illusion, but it's fascinating that our best understanding of the laws of physics *allows* for it. Perhaps time is not the forward-moving arrow we perceive it to be.

On a related matter, Einstein saw that gravity is not a "force" that keeps us on the ground, even though we experience it as such. In Einstein's theory, what we call "the force of gravity" is pictured as the effects of the actual bending of space by the Earth's mass. This is hard to picture, so physicists give us a relatable analogy. Imagine several people holding a sheet of heavy fabric by its four corners and pulling it flat and taut. If someone places a marble in the middle, it will rest comfortably atop the sheet (assuming the sheet is level). But if someone places a bowling ball in the center of the fabric, the bowling ball's mass causes the fabric to "bend." Now when a marble is placed on the edge of the fabric, it will roll toward the bowling ball.

The bowling ball is not "attracting" the marble by some "force." The mass of the bowling ball is bending the "space" of the fabric, and the marble is acting accordingly. This, Einstein showed, is how gravity works: it bends the "fabric" of space itself. And so, in this analogy, the sun is the bowling ball which warps space, and the planets are the marbles that are caught in the warpage. The bending of space is so powerful that even light bends around massive objects. And here is the real mind bender (if you'll pardon the intentional pun): because both space and time "bend" when close to a massive object, Einstein concluded that space and time are not two independent entities but together form a single space-time "fabric" that is affected by mass.

Einstein also gave us the one scientific equation that most everyone comes across sooner or later—in fact I think I remember first seeing it in an old *Mr. Peabody & Sherman* cartoon: $E = mc^2$, or energy equals mass times the speed of light squared. The fact that energy (E) and mass (m) are on opposite sides of the equals sign tells us that they are in some sense "equal"—like $18 = 2 \times 3^2$. Matter (that which has mass and takes up space) is, in a manner of speaking, "congealed energy." So when, for example, a radioactive element decays, its mass is not "gone" but is converted to energy, like heat or light. The equation $E = mc^2$ balances out—what a radioactive element loses on the m side is recouped, so to speak, on the E side. Here is a wonderful illustration from the good people at *Nova*:

> If you could turn every one of the atoms in a paper clip into pure energy—leaving no mass whatsoever—the paper clip would yield 18 kilotons of TNT. That's roughly the size of the bomb that destroyed Hiroshima in 1945. On Earth, however, there is no practical way to convert a paper clip or any other object entirely to energy. It would require temperatures and pressures greater than those at the core of our sun.[10]

So, time is relative to mass and speed, space-time bends, and matter and energy are two sides of the same coin. Not bad for a bored patent clerk.

How all this works, as I've been saying, is well above my pay grade, but some pressing questions come to mind, nonetheless, namely: *If the physical universe is really such a place that does not match my experience, can I say any less of my experiences, perceptions, and thoughts of the Creator of this universe?* How can all of this not affect how I think and talk about God?! What could (should) we imagine God to be in light of scientific theories that reveal to us a profoundly inscrutable creation? And, while we're on the topic, how does Jesus fit into all this?

We'll get to these questions in a bit, but for now, the main question is not *whether* our theology needs to be imagined differently, but *how*. Biblical scholar Dale Allison puts a fine point on it:

> If science advances through inspired exercises of the imagination—through Archimedes' association of a hot bath with the measurement of solids, through Galileo's ability to envision motion without friction, through Newton's intuition to link the orbit of the moon with the fall of an apple—then how much more our religion, which must link the finite to the infinite?[11]

Whether we realize it or not, we are always searching for ways of thinking about God that match the cosmos we inhabit. In that respect, Einstein is a key player for us. He turned on their heads longstanding notions of how the cosmos works. But this was only the first step. Einstein's insights were key factors that led to the quantum revolution, which is where things got even weirder—sometimes a little too weird even for Einstein.[12]

But weird or not, quantum physics checks out. I believe that my understanding of God can't continue as if it doesn't—and, as we'll see more clearly in the next chapter, I am actually thankful for the quantum revolution from a spiritual point of view. Amid the weirdness, God is getting bigger, for I am reminded of the marvel of creation and my human limitations. The quantum world is showing me a God who transcends every shred of my thinking on a level higher, deeper, and wider than I ever could have imagined. God is the Creator, and the creation is bringing us face-to-face with the implications of that seemingly innocent statement. That, I believe, is good news.

The Impossible and Inexplicable

One bit of quantum weirdness that physicists like to tell us about is "quantum entanglement." Everyone agrees quantum entanglement is a thing, but darn it all if anyone can really explain it. The jury is out.

It all begins with photons, which are quantum packets of electromagnetic energy (like light, microwaves, and x-rays), and *much* smaller than the 10^{-15}-meters-in-diameter protons and neutrons that make up an atom's nucleus. I'm not sure if you've ever tried to entangle photons, but I haven't, and that alone is too much for me to wrap my head around. Apparently, you take two photons and collide them. Or, if you prefer, you can also split one photon into two (?!), which would have the same effect. Either way, the result is a pair of photon "twins" that are "entangled" and moving away from each other at the speed of light—because they are photons and that's what photons do. They don't just sit there. But—and here is where things get interesting—*the twins, once entangled, stay entangled, regardless of how far apart they are.*

There is a lot more to it than that, and I seriously debated whether to try my hand at explaining more of this process, but just then, as if in the nick of time, the skies opened up, I saw a bright light, and a voice spoke unto me saying: "Pete. Don't. You'll just screw it up. Respect your readers." I agreed, and so stepped away from my desk and instead streamed the entire Marvel Avengers corpus on Disney+ before returning and just getting to the point, which is the following: the twins mirror each other's properties, but they mirror them *instantly*.

It's that word "instantly" that has physicists talking and writing long equations on blackboards. Why? Because they mirror each other instantly *no matter how far apart they are*! So what? Now it gets interesting.

As the twins move away from each other at the speed of light, years later they would be light-years apart, but they would still be entangled *instantly*. The fact that they're light-years apart in distance means they could not be communicating with each other because *communication cannot happen instantly* but must obey the laws of physics, namely "nothing is faster than light." The very idea of something faster than light would wreak havoc with everything else physicists know (and have verified countless times) about the universe—all of physics, including Einstein's theory of relativity (which has been proven), would become nonsense. And yet, the instantaneous nature of entanglement has also been verified experimentally many times. It's a fact. Photon twins, no matter how far apart, act as if they are one.[13] Wake the kids and tell the neighbors.

We are left, then, with a bit of quantum weirdness: How can the twins be in sync when they are not communicating? Physicists call this "nonlocality"—meaning, distance doesn't seem to be a factor to these twins. They act as if they are occupying the same space. Don't skim over that too quickly. It is truly weird and calls into question what we know about how everything else works in the cosmos, where space and distance matter.

One interpretation of nonlocality, which some (definitely not all) physicists hold, is that distance doesn't even exist on the quantum level. According to this interpretation, everything else in the universe behaves as if distance matters, but not these entangled subatomic particles. This suggests to some physicists that our whole idea of "space," which is where distance happens, isn't even a meaningful category on the quantum level. The quantum world exists in a "realm" (not sure what better way to put it) where distance means nothing.

Things get really interesting, and very conjectural, when someone tries to explain nonlocality (rather than simply observe that it is true)—including the explanation I just gave. We don't need to go there, and I couldn't lead you if I wanted to. But let me mention one well-respected quantum physicist, a member of England's Royal Society, David Bohm (1917–1992). He understood nonlocality not as a weirdness to be explained but as the more "basic reality" (my words, not his)[14] than our reality where space and time exist. What we call the physical world, the three special dimensions of length, width, and depth (which require space), is a projection of this other, more basic realm. What we call reality is simply an image of the deeper, truer reality—what we call reality is of this more basic reality, something like a hologram.

Not everyone agrees with Bohm, in large part because explaining nonlocality gets us into speculation that can't be verified experimentally. (And it didn't help that Bohm was blacklisted for a time as a Communist, though that is never a good reason to disagree with a scientist.) I do get and fully support that scientists need to do what scientists do and deal with evidence that can actually be tested or at least worked out mathematically. On the other hand, I am glad there have been physicists over the last century who have had an interest in asking the deeper questions of meaning and who value bringing physics and philosophy—even theology—together around the same table. For me, the need for such a conversation is a no-brainer, as long as we are willing to hold our ideas about God and the cosmos with an open hand rather than a closed fist *and* not fall into the trap of thinking that quantum physics has helped us figure God out once and for all, especially when there is little agreement on how the quantum universe works.

My guess is that nonlocality will eventually be explained scientifically rather than by a "God of the gaps" explanation, which uses the conundrums of science as alleged proofs of God's intervention. And whatever that scientific explanation may be, *that very explanation* will lead me to step deeper into the mystery of the Creator. But for now, it's enough for me to sit with the fact that quantum reality is very different from the reality we take for granted every day, and that this odd reality is part of God's creation. Perhaps another rewriting of Psalm 19 is in order: *The fact that the world of the very small behaves in impossible and inexplicable ways declares the glory of God.*

And speaking of the impossible and inexplicable . . .

Is "New Shimmer" a Floor Wax or Dessert Topping?

If "New Shimmer" rings a bell, hit me up. You're my people. For the rest of you, it's from an old *Saturday Night Live* fake commercial skit. Husband and wife (Dan Aykroyd and Gilda Radner) are in a heated argument that almost comes to blows about whether New Shimmer is a floor wax or a dessert topping. In the nick of time, in steps Chevy Chase, holding a can of the product:

> **Chevy:** Hey, calm down you two. New Shimmer is a floor wax *and* a dessert topping. Here, I'll spray some on your mop . . . and some on your butterscotch pudding.
> **Dan:** Mmm, tastes terrific.
> **Gilda:** And just look at that shine!

And on it goes—which brings us to perhaps the go-to experiment for quantum weirdness, the double-slit experiment. Here again, how things appear to us is not *at all* how they actually are. In principle that idea shouldn't sound all that odd. We perceive the sun, moon, and stars to move when in fact the earth is the one moving. We perceive ourselves sitting still though we are speeding ahead along with our car. But in the quantum world, the idea that things are not as they appear goes to an entirely different level of even asking what "matter" *is*. Individual photons, it turns out, can display both particle *and* wave behavior. It all depends on, well . . . that's what the double-slit experiment is about.[15]

Imagine a solid barrier of some sort that has two vertical slits cut into it. A light source shoots a stream of light toward the barrier and through the two slits. On the other side of the barrier is a highly sensitive screen that can detect the impact of the light after it passes through the slits. The result is that the light passes through the two slits as two waves. Those waves overlap with each other and leave a "wave interference pattern" on the detector screen.

We've all seen wave interference patterns. Drop two stones next to each other into a still pool and you see the waves emanating out and crisscrossing (interfering). Where the crests of two waves meet, they add up to an especially tall crest. Where the crest of one wave and the trough of the other meet, they cancel each other out. All waves do this, including light waves; we just don't see them with our unaided eye, hence the need for a detector.

Physicists have known for more than two centuries that light travels as a wave. If you shoot streams of photons at the double slit, they seem to go through both slits, interfere with each other, and produce the wave interference pattern on the detector. Got it? I hope so. Things aren't going to get any easier for the next page or two, but know that I believe in you.

Here's the thing. When you shoot *individual photons one at a time* (like out of a pistol) through the apparatus, you might expect something different. You might expect that each photon individually would have to go through one slit and one slit only. The detectors would then—obviously—record a particle rather than a wave pattern. And if you shot enough individual photons toward the slits, a number would find their way through one slit and others through the other slit. The detector would show an up-down pattern corresponding to both slits.

You'd think. But no. This is the quantum world.

When physicists do the experiment shooting photons one at a time, they surprisingly see the *wave* pattern on the detector. This means that each individual photon must have gone through both slits simultaneously, which makes absolutely no sense. When each *individual photon* travels through space, it acts like a *spread-out wave*, going through both slits and interfering with itself.

Well, this is truly odd, so scientists, being the clever people they are, decided to set up measuring devices by the slits to see which slit the photon is going though and basically just see what in the hell is going on. But this time (deep breath), rather than the individual photons making the weird wave pattern, they now created the expected particle pattern. Why? Good question—really good question—since the only difference between the two experiments is the presence of measuring devices that allowed the experimenters to *observe* which slit each photon went through.

It's hard for people like me to do justice to this amazing experiment, but the conclusion that at least some physicists have arrived at is right out of science fiction fantasy: the very act of measuring the location of the photon (to see which slit it is going through) somehow changes the photon's behavior from wavelike to particle-like. Some have gone so far as to suggest that the involvement of intelligent observers actually *causes* the change from wavelike to particle-like behavior. As physicist Paul Davies puts it, we are in some sense "involved with the nature of reality in a fundamental way."[16] Others are so bold to say that we actually "create" reality by looking at it, though most physicists have seemed unwilling to go that far.

Boy oh boy, do we have to be careful here and not overstate the significance of this "intelligent observer paradox," as it's called. But let's just say that performing a measurement *somehow affects* the way matter behaves.[17] However that works and whatever that means, we see nothing like that in the universe of the big. And yet this is part of the Creator's work.

Can We Wrap This Up Already?

It doesn't need to be said that I'm only skimming the surface of the surface, and by scientific standards, I'm not even doing that. But let me bring up briefly a couple of other things that get talked about at posh quantum physics gatherings.

Back to the double-slit experiment. We can't predict with precision where a photon will land on the detector screen. In the world of big things, we can predict exactly where, say, a round metal ball shot out of a cannon will land as long as we account for all the physical factors—speed, launch angle, weight of the cannonball, atmospheric conditions, etc. With photons, we have a good general idea of where they will land—a range of options on the screen somewhere. But still there is no way of predicting exactly where they will land. The possibilities are myriad, because the quantum world works with possibilities, not predictability. This is called quantum indeterminacy.

So, why exactly does this happen? I'm sort of glad you asked. Because on the quantum level, you can measure for either location or motion, not both at the same time. In our world, we can measure both, and we do it all the time. That's how we get speeding tickets. "Sir, do you know how *fast* you were going in that construction zone back *there*?" See? Velocity and position work together nicely.

But in the quantum world, the more precisely you know the location, the less precisely you know the speed, and vice versa. And so, when peering into, say, an atom's electrons, we have to choose whether we want to know the location or the speed of the electron. The more precisely we measure one, the less precise the other becomes. And by measuring the electron, we change its state. Once again, what we see is determined by the fact that it is being observed. Until observed, electrons live in a limbo of many *simultaneous* states. Deep reality is not a consistent, solid thing you can point to. It is a range of possibilities.

Let me mention one more thing, because we'll come back to it later in a different way. At the smallest level scientists can detect—at the level of individual subatomic particles—it is not at all clear what "things" are. Instead, what we are dealing with is not so much individual particles as it is the *interactions* between them—relationships, so to speak. It seems that at the smallest detectable levels of physical reality, we arrive not at the smallest *things*, but *things-in-relation*.

Newton's laws describe the motion of "things" with definite position and speed, which, apart from speeding tickets, is a wonderful thing to know. But at a more fundamental level, every "thing" is at its essence a combination of energies in a *relationship* with other things. Relationship is a big word in quantum physics, and it describes how everything . . . every *thing* . . . is ultimately connected.

More on that in a moment. To sum up: the quantum world is weird . . . impossible, actually, by Newtonian standards. I wish I understood it better, but even with my limping knowledge of it, quantum physics raises questions like, "What is reality, and how do we understand God in light of it?"—which brings us to the next chapter.

Chapter 10

Quantum God-ness

I AM MORE RELIEVED than you are that my job isn't to explain the ins and out of wave-particle duality, the intelligent observer paradox, quantum uncertainty, and the rest. But neither you nor I really needs to understand the mechanics of it all. We just need to take in the basic gist that reality isn't what it used to be.

What we assume day in and day out, and what we were dutifully taught in school, is that reality is made up of things that behave in certain ways, and that what we can perceive with our eyes is the way reality works all the way down. But that isn't the case. Barbara Brown Taylor puts it beautifully: "Reality is not a well-oiled machine that behaves in logical, predetermined ways. Instead, it is an ever-unfolding process that defies precise prediction. In it, order and chaos are not enemies but fraternal twins. Creation depends on both of them. Together they shape life."[1]

My understanding of God "all the way down" may be on no more solid ground than was my conception of time, space, and matter. But I believe it is my sacred responsibility to ask myself how my understanding of God can adapt to the universe God has made, and not in fear-crisis mode, nor even with a sense of resignation, but with a sense of curiosity, wonder, and hope for myself and the world.

That's why, as I said at the beginning of the last chapter, however much a curveball quantum physics has been for me, it is precisely the unsettling weirdness of the quantum world that has opened up for me fresh ways of understanding God. In other words, my growing understanding of the cosmos is contributing to my growing understanding of God and of the divine mystery. As I mentioned earlier in the book, how we understand God has always been in conversation—whether knowingly or unknowingly—with how we understand our world and our cosmos. The scientific issues before us today deserve the same kind of theological respect.

Part of my journey in allowing science to affect what I think about God has been paved by coming to terms with the two characteristics of the Bible that we have already looked at. The first is recognizing that the biblical writers themselves bear witness to the changing views of God that transpired over many centuries (Chapter 3) rather than presenting us with one, clear portrait of God. The second is taking to heart those mystery passages that glimpse at the reality beyond what we see, the mystery of faith and of God (Chapter 6).

Also of great help have been the voices of many theologians who have already journeyed far down that path of bringing science and religion (not just Christianity) into a meaningful and respectful conversation (Chapter 7). I am grateful to God for their provocative breath of fresh air. Among those voices is theologian Ilia Delio: "The discovery of evolution and quantum physics opened up a new window to the divine mystery that illuminates the role of God and human in evolution. It is not a matter of trying to fit the old God into the new cosmos; rather, it is the birth of a new God."[2]

I am grateful that my grip on God has been gradually loosened over the years. I have also been a bit surprised at how some familiar ideas about God and Jesus have taken on unexpected and life-giving depth and richness.

Of All That Is, Seen and Unseen

In the Episcopal church I attend, like most others, we recite weekly the Nicene Creed from the Book of Common Prayer. It begins:

> *We believe in one God, the Father, the Almighty, Maker*
> *of heaven and earth,*
> *And of all that is, seen and unseen.*

The last line catches my eye. I am not exactly sure what the fourth century writers of the creed meant by "unseen"—I assume it includes at least a nod to the angelic realm, though there may be more to it. However they meant it, I do like that they understood God to take part in what we cannot see with our eyes. What they did not have in mind, of course, is Einstein, space telescopes, quantum entanglement, and all the rest. If anyone is up for updating this ancient creed, I might suggest:

> *And of all that is, seen and unseen,*
> *a reality that turns our everyday notion of reality upside down*
> *and inside out,*
> *that leaves us with a God who is so far beyond our grasp that*
> *simply calling all of that "unseen" feels like a cop-out.*

At any rate, my own pondering of the past century of scientific revolutions has been the curveball that has also breathed new life into my sense of who God is and what "God" even means. I certainly have needed a bigger and better God than the one I had been getting far too used to over the course of my life. By "better" I mean a view of God that accounts for our understanding of physical reality rather than keeping us at a safe distance from it. The God who my informed and, I trust, sanctified (though imperfect) imagination is presenting to my mind's eye is so wholly out of my frame of reference that surrendering to the mystery of the unseen God is the only spiritual way forward that gets any lasting traction in my life.

That is the God I want—not the God of my logical deductions, not the God who behaves according to Newton-like, predictable, deterministic, cause-and-effect, theological laws, but the God I cannot control. The God beyond little old me.

I'm certainly not bashing Newton or the physical world of our senses. Newton pulled back the curtain on the realm of the seen by explaining mathematically the orbit of the planets and why things fall (which are the same thing). He had one of the most intellectually productive lives in Western history. He was a beast. But there was an unintended downside to his work. As Ilia Delio puts it, Newton ushered in "a physics of ordinary matter governed by mathematical laws rather than divine command."[3] Newton himself did not pit mathematical laws against God's commands, but that is where his discoveries eventually led. God came to be understood as something of a divine clockmaker who created the cosmos to run itself by the laws of physics and then sat back and watched it all play out.

For most of Christian and Jewish history, including the biblical tradition, people understood God to be more actively involved in how the cosmos works. But now God was not really needed to keep things running. As science continued to describe more and more of the physical world by these and newer laws, less and less room was left for God—the unseen realm began disappearing. At best, God made rare appearances once upon a time when the laws of physics were violated—what we call miracles—but now, supposedly, we know better.

Newton revolutionized physics and thus also *influenced how people understood God.* And now another scientific revolution has been before us for a century, one that has unsettled the certainty and predictability of Newton's cosmos and reminds us of the unseen, which cannot be understood by what we see and can conceive. And as with Newton's revolution, quantum physics has theological implications that have been elbowing their way to the front of the line for a century. Once again, Delio gets straight to the point: "A religion built on stability and immutability [Newton's laws] could not be prepared for a cosmic order based on change [quantum physics]."[4]

Consistency, stability, and predictability describe Newton's world of the big things. The quantum world deals in what is impossible by Newtonian standards. The unseen reality is one of unpredictability, possibility, indeterminacy. I feel my conceptions of God have to keep up—at least they need to try.

As I see it, the quantum revolution, along with evolution and cosmology, has done me a favor. Coming to some understanding of this dramatic shift in the nature of reality was something I needed to push me toward a notion that, in my mind, should need no defense, and that I never tire of saying: the God I experience here and now surpasses my understanding—not just a little bit, but in grand ways. I don't want to forget that, for when I do, I fall into the old trap of believing that God easily conforms what I see and understand. I find the God of the unseen to be wildly better.

My reluctance to think of God as a "being" (Chapter 5) is amplified by quantum physics. A God who encompasses the infinitely large and infinitely small must truly be Spirit—though even that image might suggest an "entity" floating about. As Spirit, it seems to me, God is not simply a big "thing" that is everywhere at once, but woven in and through all of reality—all matter. The best way for me to think about God at the moment is as vibrantly, energetically present in creation, from the inside out.

The view I just described is called panentheism,[5] which is made up of three Greek words: *pan* (all), *en* (in), and *theos* (God). Panentheism is the belief that God is separate from all that exists but is *in* (*en*) all things and likewise that all that exists is in God. This is not pantheism (note the missing *en*), which is the belief that God *is* all that exists—in other words, all things are God.

I am not a pantheist. I don't believe that God is the sum total of creation, but I do believe that God actively inhabits all of creation, and creation therefore is in close relationship to God. I don't worship trees or rivers, but I believe that trees and rivers exist because God's energy—or Spirit, or force, or Presence, pick your metaphor—enables them continually. Neither do I believe that God "decided" to put a tree here and a river there. Rather, I believe that God's way of creating is by the random and unpredictable evolutionary process—a process that, interestingly, resembles the behavior of the quantum world.

The unmanaged, creative openness of the cosmos yielded the countlessly diverse life-forms that have occupied this planet for more than three billion years, and has moved life on Earth toward greater and greater complexity. The crowning achievement of this process, thus far, is human consciousness. After fourteen billion years, creatures finally exist that are aware that they are aware, are conscious that they are conscious, and so can think abstractly and thus begin peering into the inner workings of the universe and come to understand a bit about the God who is responsible for it all.

I believe these things to be true, but the exact language is not a hill for me to die on. My words are more of placeholders; at the end of the day, I believe all our words are simply holding a place for that which is beyond our speech. The cosmos infused with God's Spirit continues onward; we are just trying to keep up. Placeholder theology is the very nature of theology. By it we acknowledge the human need to say something about ultimate meaning concerning the Creator and the creation while also understanding that what we say will never say it all.

In the same way that I don't dismiss Newton for describing reality only in part (which I couldn't if I tried), neither do I trash where I came from spiritually. I value my past experiences for the role they have played in my life and making me who I am, but I do not hold on to that past with a fearful grip. Since older ways are deeply ingrained in me, however, and the world around us continues to change at a steady clip, I feel my adjustments need more than a nip here and tuck there.

If I am to seek a God who does not sovereignly sit high above creation but who relationally permeates it—from subatomic particles to the largest galaxies, to the universe as a whole, or even multiple universes—I may need to rethink some things about God.

A Story About Hell

One bit of my past, however, I have fully done away with. I can no longer abide thinking of God as a being who is in a perpetual state of anger, who causes floods and dooms the stubborn to disease, or who thinks that exacting a pound of flesh for being slighted is the norm. Truth be told, my study of the Bible's ancient context has already helped move me beyond such notions, but the cosmos of the very large and the very small clinches the deal for me. Whatever lingering thoughts I might have had of a bearded (white) man up there looking down on us in a posture of judgment, however metaphorical, have become meaningless. I believe God's justice, whatever that might look like, is restorative rather than punitive—and certainly not eternal torture.

In *The Sin of Certainty*, I relayed an experience I had while watching the in-flight movie *The Bridge to Terabithia* on the way back from a fancy-schmancy academic conference. That moment has stuck with me, so I'll tell it again.

The movie tells the story of a friendship between two fifth-graders in rural Virginia, Jess and his new neighbor, Leslie. Jess is a shy and self-conscious boy from a poor and fundamentalist Christian family. Leslie couldn't be more opposite—an a-religious free spirit with a contagious imagination, who looks at life as one adventure after another. They become close friends, but Jess isn't always sure how to think about Leslie's nonconformist ideas.

In one scene, Jess and Leslie, along with Jess's spunky little sister May Belle, are in the bed of the family pickup truck in their Sunday best on the way home from church. Jess had invited Leslie, who seems to have spent her entire life insulated from the kind of fundamentalist Christian world that Jess takes for granted. But for Leslie, going to church is another opportunity for an adventure into the unknown. She is glad she came along, despite the hellfire-and-brimstone preaching, and declares, "That whole Jesus thing. It's really interesting."

May Belle is shocked and corrects Leslie: "It's not interesting. It's scary. It's nailing holes through your hand. It's because we're all vile sinners that God made Jesus die."

Leslie looks at May Belle in stunned disbelief. "Do you really think that's true?" Not only do they believe it, but Jess tells her they have to because "it's in the Bible." May Belle dutifully adds that if you don't believe in the Bible, "God will damn you to hell when you die."

Leslie will have none of it. Waving her arms as if in praise to the sky and trees passing overhead on a picture-perfect summer morning, she says, "I seriously do not think God goes around damning people to hell. He's too busy running all *this*."

As silly as it might sound, that moment in a Disney film brought to the surface something I had been nurturing deeply, away from judging eyes—that eternal torture in hell doesn't seem real or just. Leslie's words were like tumblers falling into place for me.

As I look up and ponder the cosmos for myself, I consider how it all began with one small point that has been progressing toward unfathomable size and glorious diversity, a cosmos that evolved humans with the still inexplicable quality of consciousness. When I think of that, I believe that there must be some purpose in the cosmos, even if I don't grasp it, and that this purpose is guided by God, who is love.[6] That God is love is a core Christian conviction, but the conviction has been amplified and made more real for me by a deeper understanding of the creation.

If a Creator is responsible for all this, as Leslie put it, I cannot see how this deity would have an eternal ax to grind. Rather, I believe divine love delights in creation's goodness—it tells of God's glory, to echo Psalm 19 once again. And our human response, like Leslie's, is to be drawn to God through it.

Love, I have come to believe, is God's core character trait. All other divine traits flow from love. It infuses the cosmos and will bring it to its full purpose. Those of us who get to circle the sun a few times are gifted to be a small part of that grand miracle.

Jesus at the Interstellar Bookcase

We tend to think of evolution as an impersonal process, focusing on the vastness of life and the incomprehensibility of the cosmos, which are indifferent to our tiny human concerns. Christian thinkers have proposed a way to envision how the very large cosmos and the infinitely small microcosmos are infused with love rather than detachment: Jesus and the incarnation. "For God so loved the world." A lovesick God dying to be with us.

I believe that the incarnation of Christ, though itself a mystery that I have no desire to try to parse, is nevertheless fundamental to how Christianity conceives not only of Jesus but of the very large and very small cosmos we've been looking at. Pondering the truths of the creation has led me to adjust my understanding of the incarnation far beyond Christmas Eve.

In Christopher Nolan's film *Interstellar*, Matthew McConaughey's character Cooper (an astronaut on the other side of the black hole he just went through) stares through an interdimensional library and sees his now-grown daughter Murph as a child in her childhood bedroom. Trying desperately, he realizes he can connect with her across space and time. And because Murph is the scientist who will rescue the endangered human species, this interdimensional connection will save their world. The relational bonds of love, Nolan suggests, are more powerful than the space-time limitations threatening human existence.

The relational bonds of love.

A central concept in evolutionary biology, cosmology, and quantum physics is "relationality," which I mentioned briefly at the end of Chapter 9. At its core, existence is not individual things occupying space, but things existing in relation to each other, and those larger systems or organisms are more than merely the sum of their parts. We exist as bodies because what makes us up, from the smallest components of cells to our largest organs, is a system of relationships. No living thing is simply cells thrown together but cells that work together in specific ways that yield the miracle of life—something bigger than the mere sum of its parts.

Our planet, likewise, is so relational that some in human history have spoken of Earth as a living organism (Gaia). I'm not quite ready to say that, but I get why some do. The Earth has a habit of healing itself from the likes of earthquakes, floods, and massive asteroid impacts (such as the one that likely caused the extinction of the dinosaurs and many other species sixty-six million years ago). Dare I say, the Earth will also be able to heal itself from pernicious human interference and abuse. Even recently, while humans were breaking their routines during the COVID pandemic, blue skies appeared where there had been smog, and wildlife reasserted itself in certain areas. The Earth has ways of bouncing back. Yay Earth. But if we keep up the abuse, other resets might result in the loss of human life. But that's what happens when you mess with a relational megasystem.

On the smaller scale, everything we call matter is made up of relationships, where, again, the whole is more than the sum of its parts. An atom is "made up" of protons, neutrons, and electrons—which, even though I've been saying that, isn't quite right. These elements are not ingredients added together. The atom *is* the relation these elements have to each other. Protons and neutrons in relation *are* the atom's nucleus, and they themselves are each "made up" of three smaller elements called quarks in relation to each other.

The world of the very small is a world of relationships, not discreet things that bump together. We see something analogous to this on the everyday scale as well. A cake is not made up of eggs, milk, flour, but eggs, milk, and flour in relation—meaning combining in such a way to produce something greater than the sum of its parts. There is no car without the complex relationship of the car's parts. Our social connections—churches, bowling teams, high schools, or nations—exist not as individuals occupying the same space, but as something bigger than the sum of the parts. I think of what Jesus told his disciples, "For where two or three are gathered in my name, I am there among them" (Matt 18:20). Jesus's relational presence responds to relationality.

Relationality seems to be everywhere. As theologian Denis Edwards puts it: "Nothing is conceivable as existing all by itself. There is no true being without communion."[7]

Even God exists in relationality—and now we are getting to the heart of the matter.

God Is a Relationship

Christian theologians since about the early second century have believed that God is "three in one"—one God in three persons, using the biblical language of Father, Son, and Spirit.[8] The Trinity was developed in the early centuries of Christianity, in part to account for some biblical passages where Jesus and the Holy Spirit seem to have divine characteristics. Those biblical hints were developed into some tightly woven creedal statements (like the Nicene and Chalcedonian creeds, which we touched on earlier). Thinking of God as triune is an abstract concept to be sure, and a tough topic to wade into—the Trinity is the closest thing to rocket science you'll find in theology.

So, with that, let me get to my point and lay out how I have come to see God.

The language of the Trinity is an approximation of the mystery of God, as is all our theology. But it is also a profound and unique statement about the nature of God—an approximation that points us to contemplating the mystery of God and God's relation to us and the cosmos.

I have found it very helpful to think of the Trinity as an eternally existing relationality. Let's call the three together "God," but God is not "made up" of Father, Son, and Spirit. Rather, like the makeup of an atom, God exists as the relationality of the three. The core "property" of the Christian God as this "inter-Trinitarian relationship"[9] is intimacy—a relationship of love.

Here's where this is going: *Relationality is not only at the core of reality, but at the core of God's nature. Both the Creator and the creation are relational. The creation reflects our relational Creator.*

The entire cosmos, from top to bottom is . . . well, this is where words won't do, but let me try it this way: the whole creation, from top to bottom, is God pouring Godself out, an extension of God's relationality, to create a relational universe with which God is also in relation.

Maybe God is relationality all the way down. I find this way of thinking of God very affirming of what we know of the physical cosmos. A relational God, more so than a God who sits above us in a control room pushing buttons, is a great encouragement to me spiritually.

Maybe the entire universe is a type of incarnation of God and therefore bears the divine Presence. Along those lines, it is not uncommon to hear some theologians speak of the "deification of all matter" similar to the "deity of Christ." I do want to be a little careful here, though, because these are two very different kinds of incarnations and shouldn't be collapsed together, but I see a connection between them as well.

Karl Rahner, whom we met earlier, both connects and distinguishes the two by saying that the incarnation of Christ is "the embryonically final beginning of the glorification of the *whole* reality."[10] Not a particularly clear bit of writing, to be sure, but like I said, the Trinity is an abstract concept. Putting it in my own words, Rahner seems to be saying that the outpouring of God's relational self at the beginning that gave us the universe is now intensified in another outpouring and another beginning for all of reality—the incarnation of Christ.

We get a hint of this in the Bible itself. John's Gospel begins: "In the beginning was the Word, and the Word was with God, and the Word was God. He was in the beginning with God. All things came into being through him, and without him not one thing came into being" (John 1:1–3). The "Word" (Greek *logos*) is a concept in John's day taken from Greek philosophy and refers to a divine "force" bridging the gap between God and humans. John goes on to say that this Word became flesh—Jesus. And this Word that took on human flesh and blood is the same Word that was not only with God "in the beginning" (a clear nod to the first line of Genesis) but was the one *through* whom all things exist.

John was certainly not aware of the space-time fabric, galaxies, or photons, but we are. And knowing what we know might give fresh meaning to John's words. Getting back to the Trinity, God is enfleshed in Jesus, and God is also "enfleshed" in the cosmos. God is "enmattered."

If God and creation are both relational, and if creation itself is a type of incarnation of the Creator, the bizarre idea of the incarnation of God in a first-century Palestinian laborer is not as huge a stretch, at least theologically speaking. In Jesus, God is at the very least showing concretely, at the human level, God's connection to the world of matter. As the eighth-century theologian St. John of Damascus put it:

> I do not worship matter. I worship God who made matter, who became matter for my sake and deigned to inhabit matter, who worked out my salvation through matter. I will not cease from honoring that matter which works my salvation. I venerate it, though not as God.[11]

I like this quotation because it brings Christ into the picture, which is my point in all this. Too bad St. John couldn't wax eloquent about cosmology and quantum reality, but he did a pretty decent job setting the stage for us to connect the quantum dots.

Now some of the mystery passages we looked at in Chapter 6 take on a deeper meaning for me when I see that the incarnation of God in Christ is an extension and intensification of what God was doing in creating the cosmos: "The heavens are telling of the glory of God" (Ps 19:1); "your life is hidden with Christ in God" (Col 3:3); "I am in my Father, and you in me, and I in you" (John 14:20). There is more to the incarnation of the Son than saving us from hell. Something much bigger is going on than our personal, individualistic salvation, for all of creation first passes through Christ, who is tied to all of creation: "all things have been created through him and for him" (Col 1:16).

Theology, as they say, is all metaphorical. We use words to say what words cannot express. But these are not sentimental metaphors. They are pointing beyond themselves to a grand notion, indeed: our little specks of existence are not isolated little parts of an endless cosmos, but part of a living whole that is infused with the nature of the relational, loving God.

"The world is charged with the grandeur of God," wrote theologian-poet Gerard Manley Hopkins when he was ordained a Jesuit priest.[12] Hopkins's imagery suggests that God is always closer than we think, present with us and in us along with all things. "We know that the whole creation has been groaning in labour pains until now; and not only the creation, but we ourselves," wrote Paul in the book of Romans (8:22–23). I once thought this to be a bit of rhetorical flourish to be set aside so I could get to Paul's actual theology. But I have come to see it differently: We're all in this together. All matter. All energy. Top to bottom—all humans, all life-forms, everything.

We have hope to think that our lives matter to God. The Creator is no distant monarch looking down upon us, but one who lives in us and in all matter, sustaining the creation moment by moment. Relationality is also a two-way street; one-way relationships do not exist by definition. And in any relationship, the two parties affect each other. Some theologians say that our lives matter to God in a similar way.

Our lives matter to God because our lives affect God—which is what one might expect in any true relationship.

I'm on my tippy toes here trying to see things that are hidden from me; my thinking is certainly a work in progress. But the bottom line is that God's relationality is within Godself, toward the cosmos, and toward us. We matter (an unintended but useful pun). We are not chess pieces but objects of love created by a God whose love is, as theologian Tom Oord puts it, "relentless."[13]

• • •

In a cosmos where things are not what they seem, where space bends, time is relative, matter is a form of energy, and subatomic particles have smaller components still, God is there. And we see God not despite the universe we inhabit, but precisely because of it.

This is how I think of the God of my Christian faith. There is always more to say, and the world of Christian thought has a robust history of exploring these issues head-on. All I can say is that I have gained a better understanding of God that *includes* the physical world rather than trying to explain it away or cram it into familiar ways of thinking. Maybe "for God so loved the world" is about more than just what God thinks of humans.

And this relational, relentlessly loving God, I believe, is also with me in life and in death, which brings us to a topic where things get a bit more personal.

Chapter 11

Thin Places

WE'VE BEEN TALKING a lot about the universe, how we fit into it, and how our understanding of God changes the more we ponder it. Barbara Brown Taylor weaves together beautifully the cosmos and our humanity:

> In Sunday school, I learned to think of God as a very old white-bearded man on a throne, who stood above creation and occasionally stirred it with a stick. When I am dreaming quantum dreams, what I see is an infinite web of relationship, flung across the vastness of space like a luminous net. It is made of energy, not thread. As I look, I can see light moving through it as a pulse moves through veins. What I see "out there" is no different from what I feel inside. There is a living hum that might be coming from my neurons but might just as well be coming from the furnace of the stars. When I look up at them there is a small commotion in my bones, as the ashes of dead stars that house my marrow rise up like metal filings toward the magnet of their living kin.[1]

To be sure, by pondering the cosmos, we see God and ourselves differently; frozen lion cubs, the fabric of space-time, and quantum quirkiness are causes for great contemplation about our existence. But in my opinion nothing brings us to ponder our place in the cosmos more than contemplating the end of our own existence and of those we love—and whether death is the end of it all.

Staying Curious

Death is the grand mystery of human existence and a curveball we all face. Not a curveball like the blown elbows or taxi rides, ones we do not see coming. But more like the hugeness of the cosmos and the weirdness of the quantum realm: we know they are out there, waiting for us to notice, but we seem to be able to go on as if they weren't and we won't. But sooner or later death pushes its way to the front of the line and we are forced to face it—and to ask, "Is this it?"

That question has been part of the background noise of my life since I was a child. When I was eight years old, I woke up one morning in our small apartment and strolled into the living room. When we had gone to bed the night before, the sleeper sofa had been folded up as usual, but now it was unfolded. My mom asked me whether I had slept there last night. I hadn't. Same question to my sister and dad. Same answer. Then who? Great question. Was it my cats? Did someone break into the house and take a nap? Was one of us lying? Did one of us sleepwalk? (If so, that would have been the one and only time.) My mother intuited another answer entirely. Her father had died shortly before, and she took this as a sign that he was letting her know all was okay.

During my preteen years, my European parents made occasional day trips to attend séances at a spiritual center, and I never thought much about it at first. But over time, I felt particularly tuned in to what I supposed at the time was the spirit world, which unnerved me for years. It didn't help that my parents brought home from one of their trips a book with pages of alleged photographs of apparitions. I may have been ten or eleven at the time, and this freaked me out to no end. It got to the point where I felt I was constantly sensing spiritual presences in my house and refused to go inside unless someone else was home. I was young and impressionable, so I am sure my experiences had an imaginative element to them. But I've reflected since on these experiences, and I have trouble simply chalking them all up to fantasy or trauma.

In my mid-twenties, death got my full attention for the first time. A friend's brother-in-law was killed in a car accident, an all-too-common experience in our world, but for some reason this one hit me especially hard, even though I had never met him. I think I was ready to hear it. It was time for me to count my days and thus gain a wise heart, as the writer of Psalm 90 puts it. And if wisdom needs to be kick-started by a sense of looming dread, so be it.

I was wholly shaken for weeks, obsessing over the fact that these accidents can happen at any time to any one—to me, my wife, my sister, my friends, my classmates. Anyone. I was in seminary at the time, which I suppose is as good a place as any to be grounded by the reality of the inevitable. From that point on, death had a regular place at the table of my thoughts, though the occupations of young adulthood and then midlife were able to keep those thoughts more or less at bay.

It wasn't until my late fifties that I began coming to peace with death and dying, and began pondering more deliberately what might happen when we die. I quickly concluded that I hadn't the slightest idea, clinically speaking, though there are some hints in the New Testament that seem to promise that Jesus will be the first face we see. Paul in his letter to the Philippians writes, "my desire is to depart and be with Christ" (Phil 1:23), though that has always struck me as rather short on details. I wonder if Paul's own imminent death in a Philippian jail is what flashed this thought in his mind.

Generally speaking neither Paul nor the other New Testament writers seem to be focused on the afterlife. They were more about the return of Christ to earth and the setting up of the longed-for messianic age. What happens to the dearly departed in the meantime (which was not projected to be long at all, since Christ was believed to be returning soon) was more of a side issue. So, when Paul desires to be with Christ at his death, it is not a permanent situation he envisions, but more of a holding pattern for when things go down here on Earth. As N. T. Wright puts it, the New Testament is less interested in life after death than in "life after life after death."[2]

At any rate, what began budding in my fifties bloomed as I turned the corner into my sixties. That is when I began to look at death and "Is this it?" from a place of deeper curiosity rather than resignation or reluctance. I didn't go looking for this; it just seemed like the right time. I think as we age, death taps us on the shoulder to begin the conversation. If it didn't, can you imagine? There'd be millions of old people roaming the streets in sudden abject terror. I think finding peace with death has allowed me to be open-minded about the possibility of a thin veil between the worlds, and to be ready to listen to the experiences of others—and to revisit some of my early memories from a different perspective.

So, I want to look at this grand mystery, this thing that, along with DNA, truly unites all living things, with the same sense of awe and sacred unsettledness that I view everything else we've touched on so far. And as with the other topics of this book, I am not trying to prove anything, nor am I insisting that I have arrived at a firm answer for everyone. I simply want to think about God in relation not only to the cosmos but to my place in it, and whether that place is vacated as soon as I take my last breath. I want to apply our basic principle in this book, that "our experiences affect how we think of God," by glimpsing some testimonies of paranormal (parapsychological) activity from a position of curiosity and hope. This curveball, like all the others, has been an opportunity for me to go deeper and grow, and it may be for you, too.

A Reality We Don't Often See

Not that you asked, but let me say right off the bat and without apology that I am not a scientific materialist. As much as I love science, I do not believe that what is real can be reduced to the kinds of things that the scientific method is set up to study—namely, material things, even if those material things include the infinitesimally small quantum world.

As I mentioned in Chapter 5, to believe in God is already an acknowledgment that there is more to the universe than what science can demonstrate. God is not a being alongside other beings for which we can muster testable evidence. Whatever we might find at the end of that evidentialist road would, by definition, not be God, but something within our frame of reference. And if anything, as I've been saying, the universe is shouting to me that God is not within my frame of reference. I am all in here with Dale Allison:

> Scientific materialism may be an extraordinarily productive working hypothesis, as far as it goes in the lab. That's not far enough, however, to make it a metaphysical principle that decisively settles the truth about everything, including human nature. A scientific program—Newtonian mechanics, for instance—can reveal much without revealing everything.[3]

I would only add quantum physics, which has explained much more than Newton but still not everything.

Having said that, there is an area of study that has something to say about death and life: the study of near-death experiences (NDEs) and other parapsychological phenomena. Though not a hard science in the sense of physics equations or lab tests, parapsychology is nevertheless an area of controlled, clinical study by psychologists and neuroscientists.

Some of you may be rolling your eyes at even the mention of NDEs (I can't really blame you), but the study of them and other parapsychological phenomena has, to my surprise, produced a robust academic literature that recounts truly weird things—things that cannot be explained by scientific materialist means. Not to push the matter too much, but I see a partial analogy here with quantum physics: the quantum world is real but hidden from most of us because it does not behave the way things normally do (Newtonian physics); likewise, other aspects of our existence are also hidden to most of us and cannot be explained according to our normal perceptions.

Until relatively recently, I was not aware of the pioneering work being done at the University of Virginia's Division of Perceptual Studies (DOPS). No, these are not nutty professors housed in a fraternity basement, but PhDs in UVA's Department of Psychiatry and Neurobehavioral Sciences. A nice introduction to DOPS is through an hour-long panel discussion from 2017 featuring the DOPS faculty, "Is There Life After Death? Fifty Years of Research at UVA."[4] The video description notes that DOPS work includes "studies of purported past lives, near-death experiences, and mind-brain interactions in phenomena such as deep meditation, veridical out-of-body experiences, deathbed visions, apparent communication from deceased persons, altered states of consciousness, and terminal lucidity in persons with irreversible brain damage."

DOPS's half-century of clinical studies suggests that, though hoaxes and biases certainly exist, a volume of other instances of these phenomena cannot be explained as such. Many people have experienced these phenomena, and they likely cannot be brushed aside as delusions, wish-fulfillment, or rogue brain activity. And even though we should not automatically trust anyone in a lab coat, these studies are, as I said, controlled, academic studies and subject to peer clinical review.

It seems to me that, if even a small percentage of their work is valid, it alerts us to a reality beyond what we see or understand. I can't just make believe that these studies don't exist or that they are wholly flawed.

In a March 2021 *Newsweek* article, Dr. Bruce Greyson (of DOPS) talks about his work with the well-documented parapsychological phenomenon of out-of-body experiences:

> Over the past five decades, I've interviewed thousands of people who were brought back from the threshold of death—or in some cases pronounced dead—and had striking tales to tell. Although it's impossible to say for certain what happens when we die, I have heard hundreds of accounts of people claiming to have left their physical bodies and seeing things they shouldn't have been able to see, while they were unconscious.[5]

Greyson's first encounter with out-of-body experiences was as an intern in 1973. He had a patient who had overdosed and was fully unconscious, with her eyes closed. He went down the hallway and into another room to get some information from her roommate, and then returned. The woman was still unconscious, and Greyson determined that she needed intensive care.

During his morning rounds the next day he found her drowsy but awake. He began to introduce himself when she interrupted: "I know who you are. I remember you from last night." Greyson said, "I thought you were asleep when I saw you last night." She replied, "Not in my room; I saw you talking with my roommate." Though unconscious and lying in a hospital bed, she was nevertheless present in some sense in the room down the hall where Greyson and her roommate were conferring. Greyson recalls:

> I hesitated, my mind reeling, trying to understand. Was she, with the aid of the nurses, playing a trick on me? Sensing my confusion, she made eye contact for the first time and told me about my conversation with her roommate, with details about the room we were in and what we were wearing. The hair rose on the back of my neck, and I felt goose bumps. I couldn't make sense of it, but I also had no time to think about it. I was there to deal with her mental state, not mine.

This sort of thing should not happen if we humans are simply mechanically repurposed stardust, as some say. We are stardust, but perhaps—amazingly—we are more. Of course, there will always be skeptics—we need them to keep us all honest, and they help expose true hoaxes—but when I read things like this I think . . . maybe there is reason to believe, beyond a couple of Bible verses, that we are more than our physical bodies. And if that is so, it opens the door for a reasonable reflection on the afterlife.

One other story from the DOPS video comes from Greyson's colleague, Jim Tucker, who studies purported past lives. He recounted a story of a young boy from suburban Louisiana, James Leininger. From the age of twenty-two months, James was strongly drawn to World War II–era planes. Over time he would awaken with nightmares of a fire and a plane crash. As he became more verbal, James began spontaneously relaying personal and military details of a long dead fighter pilot killed in action in World War II, James Huston, Jr. The degree of detail the younger James had of the elder defies conventional explanation. Among other things, he knew the type of plane the elder James crashed in.

And it might help to know that James's parents were conservative Christians who had no room in their understanding of God for such things as a dead person communicating somehow with their son. However, they eventually came to accept their son's experiences as true and wrote a New York Times bestseller about it.[6] Without knowing their history fully, I imagine they wound up having to adjust their understanding of God to their experiences. I can relate. In my Christian life, I never once even considered James's experience to be in any way a valid option, either.

Thin People

Before leaving this topic, I want to mention Dale Allison's work. Unlike the DOPS faculty, Allison is a New Testament historian and professor at Princeton Theological Seminary. In my circles Allison needs about as much an introduction as Adele needs in the music industry. And if my judgment means anything, I find him to be a straightforward, rigorously sober-minded, and affable chap, especially after I had a chance to share a mid-COVID-era lunch with him.

In three separate books, Allison has reflected on death, afterlife, apparitions, and other parapsychological experiences.[7] One cannot read Allison on any topic and not be impressed with the depth of his research and grasp of the material, including the history of scholarship on death and the afterlife. But he also speaks from personal experiences over which he has ruminated for decades. Here is one of them, concerning a dear friend who was in a fatal car accident:

After a few weeks in a coma, she, along with her unborn child, went away. Less than a week after the funeral, however, she came back. I was awakened in the night to behold Barbara standing at the foot of my bed. She said nothing. She just stood there—beautiful, brightly luminous, intensely real. Her transfigured, triumphant presence, which lasted only a few moments, cheered me greatly.

Then, one afternoon, several weeks after that, I was typing in my study, wholly focused on my work. Suddenly I sensed someone else in the room. The presence seemed to be located up, behind, and to my left. I understood immediately, I know not how, that it was Barbara. Unlike the first time, when I saw her and heard nothing, this time I heard her and saw nothing. She insisted that I visit her distraught husband as soon as possible. Overwhelmed by this urgent communication, I immediately picked up the phone.[8]

Allison is a famously skeptical guy. He does not claim any of his experiences as objective proof, and he is not above interrogating his perceptions. But, after many years, he still lives with the impact of those moments. I couldn't help but ask him, though, the obvious question: "Dale, why didn't Barbara just go to her husband herself? Why involve you at all, seeing as how busy typing you were at the moment?" For Dale, the answer was obvious: in the same way that ancient Celts talked about "thin places," where the realms of life and death conjoin, there are also "thin people," who are more open to such things than others.

Allison reminds his readers that these sorts of experiences are documented across cultures and across time. NDEs specifically have in fact been documented perhaps as far back as Plato. We even have one such incident in the Hebrew Bible, where the prophet Samuel's spirit is conjured up by the witch of Endor at King Saul's request. (I continue to be surprised at how otherwise literalistic readers of the Bible tie themselves into sailors' knots to explain this away.) All this leaves me wondering whether such widely experienced phenomena should rightly be called "supernatural" at all.

Those who claim to have had NDEs tend to tell similar stories, including some of the following: seeing their lives flash before their eyes; feeling a sense of being surrounded by indescribable beauty, peace, and love; experiencing a sense of timelessness; being greeted by departed loved ones; having heightened awareness; seeing a bright light (and/ or tunnel); encountering a mystical presence (God). In order to bring some rigor to these experiences, UVA's Bruce Greyson developed a sixteen-point scale to measure their intensity.[9]

Be that as it may, I am not a thin person. With the exception of my above-mentioned experiences, I have no anecdote to leave anyone gaping. I largely rely on others to enlighten me. For instance, some years ago, a high school friend messaged me. A few days earlier she had powerfully sensed her grandmother's presence saying goodbye to her. A few minutes later she got the phone call that her grandmother had just passed away. My immediate reaction was disbelief, but then I thought, "Why not? Who am I to say? What do I know about ultimate reality?"

Or here is a more recent incident in my own family. My wife had been trying to locate a children's book (*Little Bobo and His Blue Jacket*), which has sentimental value for our family. Her mother, who had died about a year earlier, used to read it to our children when they were young. Now our daughter wanted to keep the tradition alive by reading it to her children, but my wife had no luck finding it anywhere among our books, nor in area bookstores or, oddly, online. So, she thought, what the heck, let's head on down to the local thrift store (*not* the used bookstore). And there it was, right on the shelf with a few other books. My wife and daughter both felt that this might have been grandma's way of saying hi.

I've come across other stories, as I'm sure many of you have as well.

My friend Bill has had several paranormal experiences—one at the age of eight when an apparition of his grandfather appeared to him in his basement. The utter conviction of that moment has remained with him for half a century. In a recent book, funeral director Caleb Wilde recounts a "collection" (as they call it) of Noshi, an elderly man who just died at home. He and his wife were committed atheists. She told Wilde that, as Noshi lay dying, she was sitting in a "chair by his bed, watching the snow blow past the window."

> My eyes scanned the room and there, at the foot of the bed, stood
> Noshi's parents. His dad stood there on this side, and his mother stood
> on the other. . . . I talked to them, but there was no response, only a
> general feeling of warmth and goodness. . . . I was about to get up out
> of my chair to see if I could touch them, when I suddenly realized I
> no longer heard Noshi's labored breathing . . . by the time I was done
> searching for vitals, his parents were gone—along with him.[10]

It was as if Noshi's parents were there to escort him across the veil.

One more story that has touched me is that of Molly Steinsapir,[11] who died at the age of twelve in February 2021 after a bike accident about two weeks before. Her mother Kaye's amazing Twitter account (as I write this, more than 125,000 followers and growing steadily) is a testimony to a mother's sacred sorrow amid the search for hope. In one Twitter thread some months after Molly's passing, Kaye reached out to her readers asking for some solace that life goes on after we die. Hundreds of people responded with stories of their own (and I read every one of them). Many breathed the air of credibility—either that or these people were insane or pathological liars.

Like the other things I've presented in this book, I do not think I can simply disregard learned inquiry or people's experiences, even when factoring out the lunatic fringe, just because it doesn't jibe with my own common experience. Indeed, why would I want to? "There are more things in heaven and Earth, Horatio, than are dreamt of in your philosophy"—and I might add "in your theology." At least in mine.

The Good News and, for Some, Not So Much

If any of this is true, and I think some of it is, two issues are square on the table for me. The first is good news for most religious people, I would think.

Out-of-body experiences suggest a way forward in the vexing "mind-body" problem. This is a very nerdy issue that has occupied philosophers and theologians for a long time, and more recently neuroscientists, but please don't reach for the remote. This is a huge deal with potentially huge consequences.

The nature of human consciousness has not been explained yet scientifically—how did it come about that we humans have an awareness of the "self" and can think abstractly about ourselves and the universe? Figuring out why humans have this heightened consciousness is something of a final frontier. And a big debate rages.

In this corner we have the scientific materialists, who argue that our consciousness (mind) is, like everything else in our human experience, a product of our physical brains (body). When our body dies, so does our consciousness. (This view is held by Riley in the Netflix miniseries *Midnight Mass*.) In the other corner are those who say consciousness exists independent of our brains. This isn't my field, but I've read and listened to a fair amount on this topic, and I will be the first to say that I have no real professional business weighing in on it. There are serious debates to be had with a lot of moving parts, and I respect enough those doing the hard work on either side to not trample in their flowerbeds.

But still. If flatlined or unconscious people can describe accurately things they would absolutely have no way of seeing or knowing, you've got my attention. If a toddler knows details about a dead pilot he has never heard of, I'm all ears. If multiple people can testify to the same apparition, I'm not going to shout them down. I have to be open to our universe housing more than I know.

So, if these things are true, it would seem (I say this tentatively) to have something to contribute to the mind-body problem: perhaps our consciousness—which has heretofore throughout history been called the soul or spirit—exists independent of our physical bodies. Perhaps consciousness continues after death.

I assume most Christians would be more than happy to hear the news that we may very well be more than our physical existence. The second issue on the table, however, might not sit so well: *NDEs (and some other such phenomena) are reported across cultures, languages, and religious faiths.* This raises some theological questions that can't be ignored.

If people regardless of their beliefs about God share very similar— not to mention largely positive and live-altering—experiences in their NDEs, it suggests that one's beliefs do not determine one's afterlife. This is a problem because Christianity has been, at least for much of its history, very big on exclusivity: only those who believe in Jesus "go to heaven." But if these clinical studies and twenty-five hundred years of similar anecdotal evidence have any merit, Christian theology would have a reason to shift toward a more inclusive view of God.

And with that, I find myself with the same question I faced in the taxi, or my Harvard classes, or thinking about the other 99 percent of our ancestral past. Only now I am thinking about all humans ever—

past, present, and future. Are we all the same? Does God have us all in the grip of divine love?

I am happy to report that I am not the first Christian on Earth to have these thoughts. God's ultimate eternal embrace of all people is a very ancient view in the Christian church and has had its advocates throughout church history. It is well documented in the early centuries of Christianity in such theologians as Clement, Origen, Maximus the Confessor, and Gregory of Nyssa, among others. But this does not mean God turns God's back on evil and injustice. Origen (third century), for example, does not deny God's judgment, even a fiery judgment. But that judgment destroys sin and evil, not the individual.[12] The goal is refinement and redemption, not punishment. A number of authors in recent years have been instrumental in making modern readers aware of this ancient view, including Hans Urs von Balthazar, David Bentley Hart, Robin Parry, and Brad Jersak. These authors are just a small representation of the careful thought that has been given to the topic before us. Reading them is food for thought, to be sure.

Better known to many of us is C. S. Lewis, who describes a similar view in *The Last Battle*, the final book in the Chronicles of Narnia series.[13] Emeth (which means "truth" in Hebrew, by the way) is a Calormene (Islamic?) soldier who was raised to worship the god Tash and hate Aslan (Jesus). Yet Aslan grants him entrance into Aslan's Country (the afterlife), because Aslan considered Emeth's devotion for Tash as service done for him—Emeth did the best with what he knew. (Frankly, I can see Aslan/Jesus perhaps needing to grant the same grace *to Christians*, whose devotion to Christ is actually idolatry to their mixture of dogma or politics, but I digress.)

All these views together are often called "Christian universalism." God is about the business of drawing to Godself all of fractured and wounded humanity through the mystery of Christ incarnated, crucified, and raised. God will bring this about, because God's love is relentless. Moreover, because God's love is relentless, redemption does not stop at death. Like I said above, none of this means that God does not judge evil ("Hey, Hitler! C'mon in, we're good!"). But God's judgment is redemptive, not punitive, because God's love never quits.

Of course, I do not claim to know the mechanics of it all, and I certainly can't prove any of this—living with ambiguity and uncertainty is the cost of religious faith. But this is the picture of God that makes the most sense to me here and now. There is, however, a bigger circle to be drawn beyond the human drama.

A Reason to Hope

The Bible and science differ on the nature of death. In Genesis, death is an alien entity that invades a perfect creation because of Adam and Eve's disobedience. In an evolutionary framework, however, death is not the enemy of creation, but integral to it.

Death is encoded into our genes, and death is what makes evolution go. Species evolve because life-forms carrying genetic mutations that do not contribute to the survival and further advancement of the species eventually die off while the more fit pass on their genes. Death is the necessary cost of doing evolutionary business, you might say. In fact—try this on for size—this death-driven process is what allowed humans to evolve to the point where a sufficiently developed consciousness emerged that lets us ponder the meaning of death. How's that for irony?

But there is more to say about death than this stand-off between science and faith. Some theologians argue that the death-driven process of evolution reveals to us the glory of God. God did not create once upon a time long ago, one and done. Rather, as we glimpsed earlier, God's creation includes the possibility for life to emerge through evolution, a process that began with the Big Bang and continues still.

We do not live in a static, fixed cosmos with everything eternally in place. Creation *is* the evolutionary process. That includes human evolution. From an evolutionary point of view, we've done pretty well for ourselves (apart from all the incalculable harm), but "we" are not the end of the game. We are the product of evolution thus far, and like the entire cosmos, we are evolving still. Evolution is incurably forward oriented. And this should bring us hope.

When all we see is a static universe that God created at the dawn of time, our view of God will also be oriented to the past, to what God did, not what God is doing or will do. And whatever future hope there might be is imagined as a place where we *individually* meet up with other departed individuals. If that is our main line of sight, if we never fix our gaze forward and peer through the windshield, we may miss where we are going.

Some Christian theologians, such as Pierre Teilhard de Chardin and Jürgen Moltmann, want to remind us that God's location (if I can put it that way) is ahead of us, drawing us ahead, rather than drawing us back.[14] The Christian faith is, to use the fancy word, eschatological. That word has NOTHING—ABSOLUTELY NOTHING—to do with so-called end-time predictions, like the Bible is warning us about the European Union or left-wing politics. Eschatology means that the Christian faith is future oriented; God will see all things through, and all will be right. Eschatology is a central piece of Christian thinking, but Teilhard and others add a new element: we can no longer think of the future apart from what we are learning about God through evolution. Evolution is a key for unlocking what it means to speak of God as the Creator oriented toward the future.

We are moving to the future "evolvingly," not statically. Such an evolutionary future orientation is, in my opinion, a key way that Christian faith can bring hope to our world—not by calling us to maintain a fixed unyielding past that we hope to return to one day, but by looking forward to and working toward a future that the Creator is drawing us toward; and not simply a human future, but a future for all of life, our planet, and even the cosmos itself—for all of creation. Perhaps Paul in the first century already had a hint of this:

> We know that the whole creation has been groaning in labor pains until now; and not only the creation, but we ourselves, who have the first fruits of the Spirit, groan inwardly while we wait for adoption, the redemption of our bodies. For in hope we were saved. Now hope that is seen is not hope. For who hopes for what is seen? But if we hope for what we do not see, we wait for it with patience. (Rom 8:22–25)

This is how I am bringing evolution and Christian faith together. Not by squeezing evolution into familiar ways of understanding the Creator, but by asking what creation as we understand it can tell us about what the Creator is up to.

The Pattern

There is one more step we can take here, and it means bringing Jesus back into the picture, namely, his death.

The whys and wherefores of the Son of God hanging on a cross to die are things that keep serious theologians busy. Thankfully, I'm going to bypass all of that to mention just one dimension of Jesus's death that might offer a fresh perspective on the crucifixion, a perspective that, like the incarnation, connects the cosmos as a whole: death is necessary for life.[15]

As soon as the early universe cooled enough to allow gravity to congeal gases and birth stars, those stars have been dying. The process of hydrogen fusion deep inside every young star yields helium. As the star ages, the hydrogen is used up, which yields heavier elements, one of which is carbon, the crucial element for life as we know it. Producing heavier elements will eventually kill the star as it first shrinks and then explodes as a supernova, which blasts its atomic elements out into the universe. Luckily for us, those elements eventually were repurposed to make carbon-based life-forms, from the smallest bacteria to creatures like us who can ponder it all.

The death of stars is the foundation of biological life on our planet. Truly, "we are stardust, we are golden, we are billion-year-old carbon."[16] To be alive on Earth means something else had to die, and that which died was transformed into something new to make us us—and not just us, but every living thing. The New Testament also sees the death of Christ as necessary for renewed life. As it is written, "Very truly, I tell you, unless a grain of wheat falls into the earth and dies, it remains just a single grain; but if it dies, it bears much fruit" (John 12:24).

Evolution, cosmic and biological, has helped me see death from a broader perspective, as part of the cosmic order[17]—which is the out-flowing of Godself. If the cosmos reflects the nature of God, and if death is an integral part of the creation, then I might have to do some thinking about whether death is a friend or an enemy. God even gets as close to death as God can in the incarnate Son dying on the cross.

I know that Paul called death "the last enemy" to be conquered. From his point of view in human history, that makes perfect sense. In fact, who likes their mortality? "Gee, I just can't wait—if I'm lucky—to grow old, lose my senses, be a burden on everyone, and then keel over." I am not a fan of death. I am simply trying to wrap my head around how my experiences, which include science, affect how I think about death and God's role in it all.

It is said that the death and resurrection of the Son of God reflects the pattern of the cosmos itself. Life must come from death. The seed must die for something new to emerge. Death is a necessary part of the process of creation.

If death is not a punishment from God for disobedience or an enemy to be conquered, but rather is baked into the pattern of the universe, then it seems to me that this pattern is . . . well . . . universal. For all matter. For all people. And with that I am seeing a bigger God indeed.

Dealing with Reality

Some might argue that all of this theological verbiage is just a way of putting a nice face on death. I get that. Psychologist Richard Beck (channeling Ernest Becker and Sigmund Freud) has some penetrating thoughts about the neurotic fear of death that drives so many of us, especially in Western culture. In fact, Beck claims, we are absolutely *enslaved* to that fear, and so we find ways to insulate ourselves from it through "distractions, entertainments, and comforts."[18]

Western capitalism is only too willing to support this fear. We see a lot of ads, do we not, about staying young, fit, and healthy, but tell me the last time you saw an ad about burial options. We are not able to embrace the thought of death but instead create narratives in which we "fight" against disease so we can "beat death" and "survive." Beck also points out another cultural trick: to gain immortality by success, by making a mark in the world that will outlast us. Toward that end, we devote ourselves to our companies and institutions, working long hours, in the subconscious hope of living on through them. Hmm.

So, death denial is bad, and I don't want to go there, neither here in this book nor in my day to day. But understanding God and death within the framework of evolution, cosmology, panentheism, NDEs, etc., and Christian universalism is not an alternate form of death denial. It is a genuine attempt to bring an old problem into a new light, and doing so brings a dimension of hope to this normally glass-half-empty, cynical, annoyingly Teutonic nerd.

Having the presence of mind to resist our cultural tendency to live in death denial and instead have a mindset of curiosity about death can open us to a greater vision of the boundless love of God. Perhaps thinking *more* about death and listening to the experiences of others might help us gain a bigger and better God, one who inhabits not only the cosmically large and quantumly small worlds, but also each and every one of us—and loves it all.

Perhaps God's mindset all along has been to bring all of creation toward a goal that reaches far and wide, where truly *all* matter and *all* humans are sacred, "for in him [Christ] all the fullness of God was pleased to dwell, and through him God was pleased to reconcile to himself all things, whether on earth or in heaven, by making peace through the blood of his cross" (Col 1:19–20).

Einstein wrote of science:

In our endeavour to understand reality we are somewhat like a man trying to understand the mechanism of a closed watch. He sees the face and the moving hands, even hears its ticking, but he has no way of opening the case. If he is ingenious he may form some picture of a mechanism which could be responsible for all the things he observes, but he may never be quite sure his picture is the only one which could explain his observations. He will never be able to compare his picture with the real mechanism.[19]

What is true for the world of scientific discovery is true for other subjects, not the least of which is what the mystery we call God is up to in the universe.

I warmly acknowledge that I see by a dim light, and I am more than open to how others put the pieces together and to have my mind expanded or corrected. If I did not believe that—if I held on to my own thinking with a clenched fist—then I *would* be engaged in some type of death denial. But this is what I have come to believe about God.

The Christian God is more than any of our thoughts of God allow for. God, who is Mystery, is also Love, and any attempt on our part to limit that love is, I believe, not of God. A boundless God will sooner or later render all our thinking obsolete, including the words on this page. I find great peace and hope in that realization.

Chapter 12

Catching Glimpses

THE CURVEBALLS keep coming, though in recent years I am more able to recognize them for what they are—invitations to curiosity and hope in my walk of faith rather than crises to be feared and managed. Through all this I have been learning to embrace not simply my own humanity—which is itself a gift of God—but, more important, the notion that God is compassionate toward my humanity. It is not simply "okay" to allow my experience to affect how I think about God, as if begrudgingly, an unfortunate fallout of our human condition. I believe, rather, that a mature faith demands that I do so. This realization has given me the space to wrestle with some big issues that at other times in my life would have gone untended, unnoticed, or resisted, and I am grateful for this.

My path is not made of gold, and the wind is not always at my back. Nor am I a TV preacher selling a shallow faith of prosperity. Faith remains a journey, with all the ups and downs that metaphor suggests—experiencing refreshing breezes and stunning vistas as well as falling face first into ditches, slogging through mud, or contending with downed oaks blocking the way. The journey can be very difficult at times (can I get an "amen"?), sometimes so difficult it is hard to put one foot in front of the other. But it is precisely the up-and-down nature of the journey that marks it as authentic and real to me. I believe I am on the right path, not because the way is pleasant rather than hard, but because it is both.

Along the way, I am still learning to pay attention to what is happening in my world in order to catch deeper glimpses of the Creator and the creation, and my place in it. The curveballs keep coming.

You Mean, It's Not All About Me?

One of those curveballs has been coming to see more clearly my privilege as a white, cis-gender, heteronormative male. I'm not virtue signaling here or trying to score wokeness points. I am honestly confessing that I have become truly awakened to my privilege only in recent years—not in a detached way, but in an "I really get it" way.

A few years ago, I was one of several speakers at the first Evolving Faith conference (headed by Rachel Held Evans [of blessed memory] and Sarah Bessey) in rural North Carolina. One night we all decided to have a little pizza party, and I and a black male speaker were tasked with securing some adult beverages.

So we hopped into the van and headed for the liquor store. My comrade was dressed in a hoody and wore his hair in dreadlocks. When we got to the door, I was distracted for a few moments as he went inside. When I looked up, I saw the two white clerks stiffen as they eyed his every step. I may not be the sharpest knife in the drawer, but I knew this didn't look good. Not knowing exactly what to do, I just darted in, said hello, and smiled at the clerks, who responded with an expression of relief.

Not having had much experience in real-time racial tensions, I did the only thing I had in my repertoire, because I had seen it on TV. In Ken Burns's epic nine-part *Baseball* documentary, Hall of Fame announcer Red Barber recounts the taunts and slurs Jackie Robinson endured in the late 1940s whenever the Dodgers were on the road. In one instance, they were in Ohio and the crowd was particularly hostile and menacing. At one point, shortstop Pee Wee Reese, from neighboring Kentucky (hardly a bastion of racial equality at the time), walked over to Robinson at second base and simply put his arm around his shoulders, signaling to the crowd, "He's with me. Lay off."

So, that's what I did. I walked right over and put my arm around my friend and then walked with him through the aisles; we picked up the requisite supplies, paid together, and walked out.

That day, I consciously experienced my white privilege. White privilege is not an overt act of racism but the simple observation that people of white skin are historically and culturally dominant, and therefore seen as the standard or norm. As my friend put it to me, "You never have to think about your skin color; I have to think about it all the time." Whenever I am in a situation where my race puts me in the minority, I know that I can leave at any time and return to my privileged status. Others do not enjoy that privilege.

With that experience logged in my memory, I began to be more conscious of the need to look at my *faith* with curiosity and an openness to make adjustments to it. What does any of this have to do with faith? Everything. My understanding of God is not neutral but bathed in the totality of my human experience, which includes my privilege. Free of fear and crisis mode thinking, I was better prepared to be able to interrogate my faith with respect to race. I have come to understand experientially how in God's mind (if I may speak in such a crudely anthropomorphic manner) I am not remotely special, even though people of my skin color for many centuries have been more or less in charge of how the rest of the world sees the Christian God.

In my earlier years, I had had other opportunities to see God as bigger than my human condition, though it seems I was not yet ready to hear. I recall an incident in my early thirties, in the first year or two of my teaching career. After giving a lecture on the Abraham story, I was approached by several seminarians from African nations. They asked me how certain aspects of Abraham's experiences might be useful for addressing the question of ancestor worship. I remember giving a polite and in retrospect very dumb answer, about how ancestor worship really isn't the writer's intention, and we'd be better off sticking to that. On the inside, I was much more dismissive and condescending. I saw their question as a simple copping to the unexamined and unenlightened assumptions of their culture. They simply needed to get over it and learn from me what these stories are "really" about, and how we should never let our cultural biases get in the way. As if I had no cultural biases.

I disagree with my younger self on this matter, though I value that experience. I was beginning to become aware that my view of things may be tied to my privilege, which has been crowned in all its glory with an Ivy League PhD. While I will always be deeply grateful for the education I've gotten (see Chapter 2), I have also grown to see my education as a hindrance *when that perspective is seen as judge and jury of the others* (recall, again, my taxi cab moment) rather than a voice (and an important one) in a larger conversation about the Bible and its use.

I can see better now that my privilege was not simply limiting my teaching effectiveness, but my understanding of God, who is not bound by racial (or other) categories. This has been a lesson that has had to percolate slowly, in part, I am sad to say, because privilege was so deeply baked into my Northeastern suburbanite being. It took time to see it, remain present with it, and then work on extracting it. I have been shaken not only by private matters like a bent elbow or cosmic matters like galaxies and protons, but by my growing awareness of the tribalism that I had been complicit in. I would come to see that I was no different from Jonah and his deep othering of the Assyrians despite God's call to the opposite. My encoded racial assumptions were consistent with my fear-crisis model of faith, which nurtured my limited understanding of God—as limited as was Newton's cosmos compared with Einstein's.

Staying with this theme, I am more ready now to hear how deeply the tradition I have been educated in has marginalized the diversity of Christianity around the globe,[1] and how my perspective is being further marginalized as a result. My view on God is not the standard to which others must conform.

I remember a seminary professor of mine talking about how the Christian faith is like a candle that first lit the Middle East two thousand years ago, then migrated to Europe, then North America, and is now settling in Central and South America. The typical Christian today lives in the Southern Hemisphere, is of dark skin, is poor, charismatic, and female. That person's faith is not defined by the same identity markers as those in the West. African Anglicans, for example, are charismatic, have a conservative sexual ethic, and are telling liberal English Anglicans to get lost—they are in charge of their own church without Old World supervision.

And now we have our first ever pope from the Southern Hemisphere, and outside Europe, since the eighth century, who has conducted a papal mass in Spanish for the first time ever. The language of Christianity is quickly becoming Spanish, Hindi, and Swahili—not English, German, French, or Latin. The three main Christian traditions, Eastern Orthodoxy, Roman Catholicism, and Protestantism, are all largely rooted in concerns that originated in the Roman Empire. In fact, whole new traditions are emerging on the world scene that cannot be categorized neatly in any of these three main branches.

Here is something I have learned: God is not only out ahead of me, as I've been saying, but is carrying on with projects without the need to consult my corner of reality. I am being marginalized by the gospel—somewhat like the Jewish and Gentile readers of Paul's letter to the Romans might have felt marginalized at hearing how both groups, despite their tense history, were nevertheless equal in God's eyes and that neither had the upper hand. The message is now as it was then: "Sorry folks. No wall-building here. You're all humans and all in this together." I am aware of these shifts and open to them, because the model of faith I have chosen to embrace gives me the space to do so.

A Quick Glance at My Miserable Parenting Skills

My new model of handling curveballs has also helped me as a parent, though I have to say I wish I had been more aware of things thirty or so years ago when I could have used the information.

I am so very proud of my three adult children. They have each had their own challenges in life, and by them they have gained the gift of self-knowledge and emotional clarity, more than I had in my twenties and thirties (and, they will probably tell you, more than I have now). I say this even though they haven't turned out according to the Christian Parenting Script my wife and I unthinkingly signed off on more than three decades ago. For reasons different from those of Senator Bob Portman, I have nevertheless also found myself needing to make all sorts of on-the-dime adjustments to my expectations about how these three adults are living their lives and processing their inherited faith.

They were never really content to bow to the conservative iteration of Christianity that my sleep-walking-thirty-something-parent-self presented to them. Rather, they were candid enough already in their teen years to choose their own personal integrity and authenticity and say plainly what I had been too encultured not to: "What I am hearing in church doesn't match the reality I experience." It took me a while to see the simple wisdom of that observation.

My expectations of how they were supposed to turn out were not being met. But their processing of their own lives became part of my experience, in the sense that it challenged me to examine how I viewed God. Watching them brush past fear and exercise their personal agency exposed to me how I was not exercising my own. Their refusal to keep their heads down and push through brought me to question my spiritual complacency.

They have come to decide what path they will take, and all three are unique. And those paths will, I am sure, be shaped by curveballs of their own and adjustments throughout their lives. But as for me, the curveball that is "raising offspring" led to an adjustment in my understanding of God, one that seems so utterly simple and common-sensical now as I write it, but that was traumatic when I first thought it: God is not interested in church-performance and the games we play with respect to God. I came to believe, despite the loud contrary voices in my head, that God honors simple honesty more than going along with scripted roles.

In trying to be present with my children in their journeys, I came upon a related thought that would never have come to me at earlier stages of my life when operating in fear-crisis mode, and it is this: It has become self-evident to me that humans do not enter this world as disobedient rebels, worthy only of God's scorn and anger. Rather, we enter life with complex chemistries and intergenerational wounds.[2] Not only that, but—how crazy is this?!—little humans are at birth immediately subjected to being raised by marginally competent twenty-

and thirty-something humans who have not even begun to address their own complex chemistries, intergenerational wounds, and dysfunctional coping strategies, if they even become aware of them at all.

Parenting has made it very difficult to fathom something I never questioned before—that God's prime directive toward us, hyperconscious heirs to three billion years of biological evolution, is to root out and punish our rebellious hearts. I came to see a more compelling view of God by reading the contemplative monastic Thomas Keating, who refers to God as the divine therapist.[3] I know, I know. That may sound namby-pamby to some people, but that's probably because they have never been through the rinse-and-spin cycle that is called "therapy." Similarly, the Orthodox Church sees its role as that of a spiritual hospital rather than a system set up to manage a legal system of retribution. The role of the church is to be doctor and nurse, not judge and jury.

My having grown into a peaceful-hopeful model of faith over the years has given me permission to listen to those I love most in the world and be changed rather than be in immediate conflict with them so I can stay the course. I see these family moments as a pulling back of the veil to a God different from the one I had been nurturing. I do not believe we are born wicked, the sad result of the corruption of our supposed first parents (on this, see Chapter 7). We are born wounded. We need saving, but not from God's anger or from hell. We need healing from ourselves and our deep-seated dysfunction and the harm it causes. This is what I believe.

God in Christ is the healer, and that involves a process of dying of the self, as Jesus taught. What that means precisely as we take our laps around the sun is something I am happy to continue fleshing out in the few laps I have left. My point, though, is that a model of faith marked by curiosity and a conviction that the Creator is not out to get us has changed my life. I am not losing sleep over whether or not my children are saved in a conventional evangelical sense. Instead, I try my hardest to be to them the loving, caring, and healing presence God has modeled for me. I am grateful that my thinking has changed. I would hate to think of passing my years in conflict with my own flesh and blood fueled by fear and crisis thinking.

Performance Art

Quick confession: I've never been excited about church. Yeah, I said it. As a kid, I would begin taking my church clothes off in the front yard and be in my shorts and T-shirt before the rest of the family had made it out of the car.

Hear me out. I am not against church. I'm just being honest that I have always felt church attendance to be performative—like a box that needed to be checked off as a way of making sure I kept up appearances. That's all me, which is my point in this mini-rant. In my adult life, I have come to understand that at least some of my feelings about these duties stem from my introversion and my emotionally protective tendency to avoid intimacy. That's all I'm going to say about that, but if you want more, you are more than welcome to try to bribe my therapy team.

Anyway, my point is that in my later years, I have been able to explore this part of my life rather than simply push through the bracing oncoming wind, thinking that as long as I keep trudging along without complaint, it will eventually all turn out fine. I just have to be honest and say that going to church on Sunday has not been the most grounding spiritual experience of my life—and biblical proof-texts about why it should be don't work (so please hold your emails and social media comments).

But here is an area of my life, I would say a very important one, where a more compassionate model of faith is saving me. Rather than playing the game, I can actually look at my situation honestly without fear or holding fast to a predetermined conclusion. And that path only became clear to me several months ago.

A close friend of mine is in Alcoholics Anonymous and invited me to a meeting. I had never been to one, but I know others who have said they get more out of those meetings than church. I was about to experience what they meant.

Different meetings do things differently (like churches!), but this one had a familiar rhythm. It began with some announcements, the reciting of the twelve steps, and then going around the room with each person reading an assigned portion from the AA "Big Book." I felt like I was in a Bible study. The only thing missing was the forty-five-minute evangelistic lecture-sermon, which you will never find in AA. They don't lecture. They bare their souls.

The meeting then turned to a lengthy discussion of Step 11, which deals with the role of meditation and prayer in recovery. Hearing people in this "church" struggle openly, honestly, and vulnerably with prayer and meditation was amazing. Such wisdom born of life experience and suffering! No one was posturing to see who knew the most, which is where my head goes when I am asked to speak in church or chime in during a Bible lesson. "AA isn't so much about alcoholism, but crushing the ego," as my friend told me. I long for that kind of authentic community.

All experiences were valued, none dismissed, even though there were clear disagreements. The point of the meeting was not to make sure everyone had the same correct view. My friend explained, "We don't have time for that bullshit. People are trying to survive." The group shared truly about their struggles and received encouragement, support, and guidance from their fellow strugglers. The measure was not what is "right" or the "correct view," but what was helpful, what was needed for the moment. (If I may add, addressing the needs of the moment is very much the mindset that explains the diversity we see in the Hebrew Bible and New Testament; see Chapters 3 and 4.)

The meeting created a safe place where people felt anchored in a community of support. I left with a fresh vision for what church could be and frustrated that I had never experienced such a thing in all my years of attending church and as a seminary professor preparing others to lead. If only these kinds of discussions could happen more often in churches, I think we would find people flocking to their doors—or at least be a bit less likely to keep away from them.

My point here is simply that I am able now to explore what church means for me, not as an exercise in self-absorption or spiritual rebellion, but because I believe this is what God wants of me.

I believe the life of faith requires us to know ourselves, to do an honest personal inventory on a regular basis. Long ago, John Calvin began his magnum opus *The Institutes of the Christian Religion* remarking on how knowledge of God and of self are intertwined.[4] I am not suggesting he meant exactly what I do, but our concerns certainly overlap. My own sense of God's Presence had been adversely affected for many years because I did not have sufficient knowledge of self in order to listen to that inner voice telling me something was wrong; instead, I just ignored it. Honesty made me feel much closer to God than going through the motions ever did. Is this sort of honesty and making of adjustments not vital for any sort of relationship we find ourselves in?

A rigorous personal inventory can be intimidating because we sense something will need to change. But we do it in order to keep moving forward and not mistake the way things are for the way they can be. I am respectful of my past, but I am also keying in to new experiences, which push me to see how I might experience a bigger and better God.

I've had a similar process concerning traditional prayer, which has never felt natural to me. It, too, feels like a performance, a box to check off and keep up appearances—and public prayer just makes it worse.

I've been able to be honest with God and myself about prayer, too, and as a result my impulse to pray has been nudged in directions I would not have recognized in years past, when I was trying to conform to what people considered normal and was fearful if I was out of step.

Rather than trying to figure prayer out all at once, I've decided to keep it simple and just work on being thankful—even though when I stop to think about thankfulness, my mind starts turning. I mean, what does it mean for me to be thankful for my family when others have no family or have lost their family? Or the same with a home, income, health, etc.? If I think it through, thankfulness can feel narcissistic, but I decided to plow ahead anyway, not because I have figured it out, but because I want to acknowledge in some practical way my belief that God is in all and through all and with all.

I am not so much thanking God for "giving me" this, that, or the other thing, as if the God of two trillion galaxies and quantum entanglement moonlights as my personal patron deity. I'm just trying to acknowledge that my existence is derivative of the One by whom all existence is possible. I am giving thanks to the one in whom "we live and move and have our being," to quote Paul (Acts 17:28). As philosopher David Bentley Hart puts it, "[God] is the one reality in which all our existence, knowledge, and love subsist, from which they come and to which they go, and that therefore he is somehow present in even our simplest experiences of the world, and is approachable by way of contemplative and moral refinement of that experience."[5]

Our existence and everything we experience is from God because God is the sole source of all existence. And so I thank God.

• • •

Writing some of the words in this chapter and throughout this book would have paralyzed me years ago. Like my Maytag moment in 1989,

I would have had to steel myself against that inner voice of judgment, guilt, and shame for having strayed so far from the unchanging "truth."

And so, this book as a whole is in a true sense an expression of thanks to the Creator of all reality for my experiences, from blown elbows to galaxies and photons. Through them I am in a much better place.

What If?

At the end of the day, I think all this believing, praying, studying, and the rest is simply about wanting to know God and be known by God. I think that is what we are after—at least I know I am. The question is how to get there. Devising a packaged step-by-step plan has never worked for me, and I suspect the infinite Creator of all existence is not overly impressed with our attempts to commodify a search for ultimate meaning in the universe.

I do see a clear way forward, and it is not at all complicated, even though it may appear difficult at first. It amounts to a change in attitude in how we approach the life of faith.

What if the way to God thrives by allowing our experiences in life to have their say?—from the mundane to the cosmic and everything in between. What if the experiences of our lives in this evolving cosmos are a gift to help us see a bigger and better God, rather than a long exam to prove ourselves worthy? And when our lives bring anguish and suffering, what if a gentle way can be opened to us to see them also moving us toward a bigger vision of what we mean when we talk about God?

What if we are meant to live free from fear concerning God? There are plenty of other legitimate fears and sufferings we deal with in the course of our lives. What if God isn't one of them? What if part of the gift of life, and of the advanced consciousness we have, is to become more and more aware of the Source of All Being, the divine Presence all around us, the Creator who is present in every atom and subatomic particle in all of creation?

And what if *all* of our experiences, not just the Bible-reading and church-going parts, are telling us to look up from those moments and crane our necks toward the sun in order to grow in the knowledge and love of God? And what if those experiences include not only the cosmic and major turning points of our lives, but the very mundane and everyday moments that actually make up most of our existence?

What if God the Creator is ever-present in and around us, and every waking moment of our lives is an opportunity to grasp a slightly thicker sense of the Infinite Mystery? What if this is what God is like? What if this is what God desires for all of us?

When our faith takes turns we never saw coming, when what made sense before makes little sense now, we are in that sacred space of having to decide whether or not we will adjust to the curveball. And what we decide will make all the difference.

ACKNOWLEDGMENTS

First of all, and lest I forget, as per usual Marmalade's pawing and purring antics delayed delivery of this book by several weeks—though she did point out some blind spots and offered several helpful corrections.

Speaking of corrections, this has been a different sort of book for me to write, and as such I found myself needing more adult supervision than in past efforts. In particular, I asked several learned friends to read the manuscript at various stages to make sure that I, in a flurry of enthusiasm, didn't overstate or flat out misunderstand the science. Others were kind enough to confer with me on some of the theological issues that invariably come up when talking about science—not to mention God, Jesus, and the rest. So, I give my deep and sincere thanks to Ben Byerly, Eric Flett, Tripp Fuller, Loren Haarsma, Walt Huddell, Mike McHargue, Bill Meinel, Nick Menzies, Tom Oord, Rick Schaeffer, and Peter Wall.

A special shout-out to my agent, Kathy Helmers, who tirelessly and with only a hint of sarcasm helped me stay on track and offered all sorts of great ideas about how to actually make sense to my readers. My editor, Mickey Maudlin, along with his wonderful team at HarperOne, as always, offered insights I was blind to and which helped make this book more lucid than it would otherwise have been. My friends and former students Ally Bartlett Ruch and Maddie Ridgeway read an earlier draft and absolutely loved every single word of it, except those places where they told me to change it up completely. Tanya Lee was kind enough to read through the manuscript in its final stages and saved me from numerous grammatical infelicities. My assistant, Ashley Ward, who continues to be my day-to-day adult supervision, took a pile of work off my desk to make sure I had time to read and write. My *Bible for Normal People* colleague Savannah Locke's creative energy toward the end of this project is greatly valued and appreciated.

I am thankful to my full-time employer Eastern University for granting me a full-year sabbatical in 2021–2022 to write this book. I have never written anything before without also shouldering academic responsibilities, so my sabbatical year was wonderful—a glimpse of heaven, you might say, or at least retirement. I plan on talking my provost into letting me be on sabbatical every year. I'll keep you all posted.

I dedicate this book to my second grandchild, Beau James Petters, who was born a couple of months before I started seriously working on this book. A "Generation-C" baby, his first two years of life were spent in COVID protocols, and I suspect he will grow up in a world very different from the world I knew in my youth. In time, perhaps he might find some echo of hope in this book. In the meantime, he will probably keep dismantling appliances, disturbing the peace, locking his mom out of the house, eating everything in sight, napping only when he wants to, teasing his older sister, letting grandpa tickle him and play alligator pit, and generally just laughing and smiling through life, undeterred by crushing social norms and expectations.

You do you, Beau.

Notes

Chapter 1: My True Purpose. Or Not.

1 This means nothing if you're not into baseball, but it's a way of gauging how many outs a pitcher gets by striking batters out. Nine strikeouts per nine-inning game is pretty good. I averaged more than twelve, which is still a record for my college nearly forty years later. To impress you further, my other college record of note is wild pitches. I was more interested in blowing the ball past batters without caring much about where it went. Some have suggested these extremes are a metaphor for my emotional life.

2 I came to learn later that scouts generally sign players who they feel will be major leaguers within a few years (say by age twenty-four or twenty-five), not because they are good enough to pitch in the minor leagues now. The scouts felt I was good but not good enough to take a chance on.

Chapter 2: I Love You, Bible. Just Not "That" Way.

1 The Christian Bible certainly contains sections that contradict each other. In the Hebrew Bible, one need only compare the different accounts of Israel's monarchy as we read them in 1 and 2 Samuel/1 and 2 Kings and then in 1 and 2 Chronicles. In the New Testament, we have four Gospels that clearly (and intentionally) differ from each other. The reason for such a state of affairs is not confused authors, but the fact that the biblical authors wrote at different times and places, and under different circumstances—not to mention viewed the world through their own distinct lenses. Peter Ens, *The Bible Tells Me So: Why Defending Scripture Has Made Us Unable to Read It* (San Francisco: HarperOne, 2014); Ens, *How the Bible Actually Works* (San Francisco: HarperOne, 2019).

2 The exploits of King David, for example, seem to be mimicked in the earlier tales of Abraham and Judah. For example, the political relationship between the kingdoms of Israel and Edom is oddly reminiscent of the relationship between their eponymous ancestors Jacob and Esau.

3 This analogy comes from Gary Rendsburg's essay "The Genesis of the Bible." For a fuller and more academic take on this, see Gary A. Rendsburg, *How the Bible Is Written* (Peabody, MA: Hendrickson, 2019), 443–67.

4 The quotation is from Joseph Ratzinger, *Jesus of Nazareth: From the Baptism in the Jordan to the Trasfiguration*, trans. Adrian J. Walker (New York: Doubleday, 2007), 97–98 (italics added).

Chapter 3: Welcome to a New Normal

1 Not to complicate things unnecessarily, but dating the beginning of Israel's monarchy to 1000 BCE is problematic. Saul and then David were more warrior-leaders trying to wrangle together various groups than kings reigning over a united land. In fact, many scholars think that there never was a united monarchy that eventually spilt into northern and southern factions (around 930 BCE). If we take the United States of America as a modern analogy, it would be like saying that there never was a "United States" that split during the Civil War. Rather, North and South always saw themselves as distinct, as did the individual states, which governed themselves. In this scenario, the idea of a presplit "United States" was only imposed by the North after it won the war as a way of bringing some unity to the country. Of course, this didn't happen, but it is roughly how some scholars understand the united monarchy over a united Israel—it is more propaganda than historical fact. It is also worth noting that the earliest evidence we have from outside of the Bible for Israel's politics comes from the ninth century BCE, when the northern and southern factions existed. If we ever uncover clear archaeological evidence for a united monarchy, the scholarly portrait will need to be adjusted accordingly.

2 It might be worth knowing that "forever" is the Hebrew word *'olam*, which does not mean a literal eternity, as Christians typically presume. It means more a long duration that can extend either backward or forward in time. David's "forever" reign would be through his children and would last a "good long time." The notion that, according to the New Testament, David's descendant Jesus will reign forever should not be read back into the Hebrew Bible.

3 I gleaned this term from James L. Kugel, *The Great Shift: Encountering God in Biblical Times* (Boston: Houghton Mifflin, 2017), 169–75.

4 I explore this idea at greater length in *How the Bible Actually Works*.

Chapter 4: Adjusting for Jesus

1 Ancient Judaism was not a monolith. Various groups emerged that responded differently to cultural shifts, and especially to Greek and Roman occupation. Four of those groups are known to us: the Pharisees, Sadducees, Zealots, and Essenes—all but the last of which are mentioned in the New Testament. The Pharisees tended to resist the idea of Roman influence and were more concerned with the interpretation of the law of Moses. Sadducees were of the upper class of Jewish society and were in charge of the temple. They welcomed the power given them by Roman rule. The Zealots, by contrast, were all about rebelling against Roman rule. The Essenes, according to other ancient sources, were more of a separatist group that removed itself from society and practiced asceticism. They are also likely the group that is responsible for the famous Dead Sea Scrolls, which were discovered in 1946–1947. Apart from these four groups, other opinions were likely floating around among the common people about how to live with the Romans, including simply wanting to be left alone to live their lives.

2 The wicked King Antiochus IV Epiphanes (215–164 BCE) persecuted the Jews, which led to a Jewish revolt in 167 BCE, memorialized in the Hanukkah celebration. The persecution ceased in 164 BCE, but not before the blood of many faithful Jews had been shed. The anonymous author of 4 Maccabees says of these martyrs: "the tyrant [Antiochus] was punished, and the homeland purified—they [the martyrs] having become, as it were, a *ransom* for the sin of our nation. And through the blood of those devout ones and their death as an *atoning sacrifice*, divine Providence preserved Israel that previously had been mistreated" (4 Macc 17:21–22; emphasis added). "Ransom" and "atoning sacrifice" also describe Jesus's crucifixion in the New Testament, for example, Mark 10:45 and 1 John 4:10.

3 John's Gospel begins, "In the beginning was the Word, and the Word was with God, and the Word was God. He was in the beginning with God. All things came into being through him, and without him not one thing came into being. What has come into being in him was life, and the life was the light of all people" (John 1:1–4). "Word" is a concept borrowed from the world of Greek philosophy. The Greek term is *logos*, and grasping its exact meaning can be tricky. It often means something like logic, reason, or divine thought or plan. In some Jewish circles influenced by Greek thought, "Word" was the divine "force" of creation as well as a divine mediator bridging the gap between God and humans. For John, the Word, who was with God at creation and through whom all things were created, is the same Word who "became flesh and lived among us" (John 1:14).

4 A list of worldwide Christian denominations can be found at Wikipedia, "List of Christian Denominations by Number of Members," Wikipedia, last updated September 22, 2022, https://en.wikipedia.org/wiki/List _of_Christian_denominations_by_number_of_members. According to the Center for the Study of Global Christianity (CSGC) at Gordon-Conwell Theological Seminary, the total number of Christian denominations worldwide runs as high as forty-one thousand, though "this statistic takes into consideration cultural distinctions between denominations in different countries, so there is an overlapping of many denominations" (Mary Fairchild, "How Many Christians Are in the World Today?," Learn Religions, last updated April 16, 2020, https://www.learnreligions.com /christianity-statistics-700533). The true number is certainly far less than forty-one thousand, but even four thousand or four hundred would make the point.

Chapter 5: Blink of an Eye

1 I first saw this quotation in Dale Allison, *The Luminous Dusk: Finding God in the Deep, Still Places* (Grand Rapids, MI: Eerdmans, 2006), 2. This quote struck an immediate and deep chord with me.

2 See Bob Berman, "The Ever-lasting Question: More Sand or Stars?," Astronomy, January 23, 2019, https://astronomy.com/magazine/bob-berman /2019/01/more-sand-or-stars.

3 Although space is not really empty. Astrophysicists are on the search for dark matter and dark energy, which cannot be seen by any means we have available to us but which mathematically have to be there. On dark matter, see Richard Panek, *The 4 Percent Universe: Dark Matter, Dark Energy, and the Race to Discover the Rest of Reality* (New York: Houghton Mifflin Harcourt, 2011).

4 Blaise Pascal, "Of the Necessity of the Wager," sec. 3, nos. 205 and 206, in Blaise Pascal, *Pensées*, trans. W. F. Trotter, Christian Classics Ethereal Library, https://ccel.org/ccel/pascal/pensees/pensees.

5 Nicolaus Copernicus (1473–1543) created a scientific model that put the sun at the center of the solar system rather than the Earth. Galileo Galilei (1564–1642), among other things, is known for getting in hot water for his support of Copernicus's heliocentrism. Johannes Kepler (1571–1630) developed laws of planetary motion, mathematically working out the elliptical (rather than circular) revolution of the planets around the sun.

6 Wordsworth's words are cited in Allison, *The Luminous Dusk*, 85–86.

7 A number of books in the bibliography represent a small sampling of the work that has been done in recent years and from which I have learned much, including but not limited to work by Anna Case-Winters, Denis Edwards, John

Haught, Ilia Delio, John Polkinghorne, Tom Oord, and Thomas Torrence. I would also like to mention the series John Robert Russel, ed., *Scientific Perspectives on Divine Action*, 5 vols. (Vatican City State: Vatican Observatory Publications/Berkeley, CA: Center for Theology and Natural Sciences, 1993–2001), which is an invaluable five-volume collection of essays covering quantum cosmology, chaos theory, evolution, neuroscience, and quantum mechanics.

8 See Peter B. Todd, *The Individuation of God: Integrating Science and Religion* (Asheville, NC: Chiron, 2017).

9 See "The Pillars of Creation," NASA, February 22, 2018, https://www .nasa.gov/image-feature/the-pillars-of-creation.

10 David Bentley Hart comments eloquently that such a view of God is hardly innovative but is central to the "great theistic traditions," namely, "orthodox Judaism, Christianity, Islam, Sikhism, Hinduism, Baha'i, a great deal of antique paganism, and so forth." David Bentley Hart, *The Experience of God: Being Consciousness, Bliss* (New Haven, CT: Yale University Press, 2013).

> God so understood is not something posed over against the universe, in addition to it, nor is he the universe itself. He is not a "being," at least not in the way that a tree, a shoemaker, or a god is a being; he is not one more object in the inventory of things that are, or any sort of discrete object at all. Rather, all things that exist receive their being continuously from him, who is the infinite wellspring of all that is, in whom (to use the language of the Christian scriptures) all things live and move and have their being. In one sense he is "beyond being," if by "being" one means the totality of discrete, finite things. In another sense he is "being itself," in that he is the inexhaustible source of all reality, the absolute upon which the contingent is always utterly dependent, the unity and simplicity that underlies and sustains the diversity of finite and composite things. Infinite being, infinite consciousness, infinite bliss, from whom we are, by whom we know and are known, and in whom we find our only true consummation. All the great theistic traditions agree that God, understood in this proper sense, is essentially beyond finite comprehension.

Chapter 6: Just When You Thought You Had the Bible Figured Out

1 In some of my previous books, I look more deeply at the Bible's ancient weirdness as signposts for truly grasping what the Bible is and what it means for us to read it well. Peter Enns, *Inspiration and Incarnation: Evangelicals and the Problem of the Old Testament*, 10th anniversary ed. (Grand Rapids, MI: Baker, 2015); Peter Ens, *The Bible Tells Me So*; Ens, *How the Bible Actually Works*.

2 Abraham Heschel quoted in Jon D. Levinson, *Creation and the Persistence of Evil: The Jewish Drama of Divine Omnipotence* (San Francisco: HarperCollins, 1988), 63. Levenson is citing Abraham Joshua Heschel, *God in Search of Man: A Philosophy of Judaism* (New York: Harper & Row, 1966), 46.

3 Barbara Brown Taylor explores this theme in *Learning to Walk in the Dark* (San Francisco: HarperOne, 2014), and *The Luminous Web: Faith, Science and the Experience of Wonder* (London: Canterbury, 2000), as does Dale Allison in *The Luminous Dusk*.

4 As regards how much we can know, I love the following quotation from Allison, *The Luminous Dusk*, 173–74 :

> I find it helpful in this connection to think about my dog Ralph, who is more German shepherd than anything else. Ralph knows that his food is kept in a large bag in the kitchen cabinet, and also that when I go to that cabinet with his dog bowl in hand, he is about to enjoy a meal. That is why he then barks with excitement. Ralph further knows that rubbing his large paws and whiskered nose against the cabinet in my presence communicates hunger, and that turning over his empty water bowl will get it filled immediately. Regarding his food and water, then, Ralph can think well enough.
>
> There is, however, a fixed limit to his understanding. He does not know that bags of dog food come from a grocery store, a thing for which he has no concept. He does not know that a store has products because there are trucking lines. And he knows nothing about the agricultural operations or the manufacturing processes that result in bags of food. Such knowledge is too high for him; he cannot attain it.
>
> These are things, moreover, that he can never understand. I could spend every waking hour trying to instruct him about the long chain of events that puts dog food in the kitchen cabinet. But it would all be in vain, for his mind is constricted. Beyond a knowledge of certain facts about the cabinet and his bowl, there is only fog. His mind runs out.
>
> So too must it be with us. Some of us seem to imagine that because we understand much, we should be able to understand everything, and that science will continue pulling up the blinds, exposing to the light more and more of the dark room that is our ignorance. But this is a faith one need not be embarrassed to decline. Despite all our knowledge about ourselves and the universe we inhabit, much more is unknown than is known; our ignorance drowns our knowledge; and, just as Ralph's understanding soon enough meets what it cannot fathom, so too is it with us. The world is large, and our minds are small, so the latter cannot always contain the former. We cannot but expect there to be mysteries— permanent mysteries—on every side.

5 David Bentley Hart has many incisive thoughts on this topic in *The Experience of God*, none less so than the following (which appears on p. 332): "More simply, we shall arrive at a way of seeing that sees God in all things, a joy that encounters God in the encounter with all reality; we shall find that all of reality is already embraced in the supernatural, that God is present in everything because everything abides in God, and that God is known in all experience because it is the knowledge of God that makes all other experience possible."

6 C. S. Lewis, *Mere Christianity* (London: Macmillan, 1952), 174.

7 Mark William Worthing, *God, Creation and Contemporary Physics* (Minneapolis: Fortress, 1996), 201.

8 Karl Rahner, "The Spirituality of the Church of the Future," in *Theological Investigations, Vol. 20: Concern for the Church*, trans. Edward Quinn (New York: Crossroad, 1981), 149.

Chapter 7: The Other 99 Percent

1 David Kindy, "Near-Perfect Cave Lion Cub Corpse Found in Siberian Permafrost," *Smithsonian Magazine*, August 10, 2021, https://www.smithsonianmag.com/smart-news/near-perfect-cave-lion-cub-corpse-found-siberian-permafrost-180978403/.

2 See Geoffrey Migiro, "The Oldest Ships in the World," WorldAtlas, May 21, 2018, https://www.worldatlas.com/articles/the-oldest-ships-in-the-world.html; see "Ancient Maritime History," Wikipedia, last updated September 19, 2022, https://en.wikipedia.org/wiki/Ancient_maritime_history; see "History of Wrestling," Wikipedia, last updated July 30, 2022, https://en.wikipedia.org/wiki/History_of_wrestling; see "History of Beer," Wikipedia, last updated September 16, 2022, https://en.wikipedia.org/wiki/History_of_beer.

3 See Andrew Curry, "An Immense Mystery Older than Stonehenge," BBC, August 16, 2021, https://www.bbc.com/travel/article/20210815-an-immense-mystery-older-than-stonehenge; see "Stonehenge," History.com, last updated February 19, 2020, https://www.history.com/topics/british-history/stonehenge.

4 See Brian Handwerk, "An Evolutionary Timeline of Homo Sapiens," *Smithsonian Magazine*, February 2, 2021, https://www.smithsonianmag.com/science-nature/essential-timeline-understanding-evolution-homo-sapiens-180976807/.

5 Darwin's classic *On the Origin of Species* was published in 1859, and *The Descent of Man* in 1871; See Charles Q. Choi, "How Did Multicellular Life Evolve?," Astrobiology at NASA, February 13, 2017, https://astrobiology.nasa.gov/news/how-did-multicellular-life-evolve/; See Handwerk, "An Evolutionary Timeline."

6 *The DNA Tests,* "How Much DNA Do Humans Share with Other Animals and Plants?" https://thednatests.com/how-much-dna-do-humans-share-with -other-animals/.

7 Recently, apologist William Lane Craig, *In Quest of the Historical Adam: A Biblical and Scientific Exploration* (Grand Rapids, MI: Eerdmans, 2021), has thrown his hat in the ring on this option. He argues that Adam was not the first human but a member of the early human species *Homo heidelbergensis* and lived between 750,000 and 1 million years ago. Craig is known for his defense of biblical authority, and I find his claim a welcome, surprising, and significant concession to scientific fact, for which he is to be applauded, particularly given his conservative readership. On the other hand, his insistence in retaining a notion of biblical authority that requires a literal Adam of some sort, even a *Homo heidelbergensis* man, seems to minimize the Bible's ancient Near Eastern context and the rise and evolution of religions in general.

8 For some hefty reading, see Kieth B. Miller, ed., *Perspectives on an Evolving Creation* (Grand Rapids, MI: Eerdmans, 2003), and Robert John Russell, William R. Stoeger, and Francisco J. Ayala, eds., *Evolutionary and Molecular Biology: Scientific Perspectives on Divine Action* (Vatican City State: Vatican Observatory/Berkeley, CA: Center for Theology and the Natural Sciences, 1998). For something more accessible, see the books listed in the bibliography by Denis O. Lamoureux.

9 St. Augustine, *The Literal Meaning of Genesis,* trans. J. H. Taylor, 2 vols. (New York: Paulist, 1982), 1:42–43.

10 Johnathan Sacks, *The Great Partnership: Science Religion, and the Search for Meaning* (New York: Schocken, 2011), 352–3.

11 *Yellowstone,* season 4, episode 5, "Under a Blanket of Red."

12 Technically speaking, "evolution" is limited to biology and involves genetic change over time. When we speak of the evolution of the cosmos or of the Earth, we are using the term as a metaphor for a nonstatic cosmos and Earth. But even having said that, there is somewhat of a connection between the scientific and metaphorical meanings. The revolution of biological evolution in the nineteenth century developed in the wake of the geological evolution one to two centuries earlier. The Earth's crust emerged over time from volcanic activity and earthquakes, and sedimentary rocks reveal ancient layers of the Earth; Ilia Delio, *The Unbearable Wholeness of Being: God, Evolution, and the Power of Love* (Maryknoll, NY: Orbis, 2013), xvii.

13 Many other cosmologists, informed by quantum theory, theorize that our universe is one of limitless others that bubbled up (my words) and out of another universe in an endless cycle of universes. From what I can tell, this view is gaining traction. One universe is more than enough for me to get my head around, so I'm just going to leave this here.

14 Richard B. Larson and Volker Bromm, "The First Stars in the Universe," *Scientific American*, January 19, 2009, https://www.scientificamerican.com /article/the-first-stars-in-the-un/.

15 Ethan Siegel, "The Only Three Heavy Elements in the Universe That Aren't Made in Stars," *Forbes*, July 1, 2015, https://www.forbes.com/sites/ethansiegel /2015/07/01/the-only-three-heavy-elements-in-the-universe-that-arent-made -in-stars/?sh=b3a49db39e68.

Chapter 8: Other People (Eww. I Mean, Yay.)

1 Scholars call these four books the "Johannine literature" for sake of reference, even though many see no reason to think the disciple John wrote them. "Johannine" is from the German "Johan" since "John" is virtually impossible to turn into a decent-sounding English adjective (Johnian?!). The other Gospels can form fine English adjectives: Markan, Matthaean, and Lukan.

2 A wonderful look at navigating love in contentious contexts is Jared Byas, *Love Matters More: How Fighting to Be Right Keeps Us from Loving like Jesus* (Grand Rapids, MI: Zondervan, 2020).

3 For Rohr's tricycle metaphor, see Richard Rohr, "Another Way to See the Bible: Lesson 4, The Tricycle: Scripture, Tradition, and Experience," Center for Action and Contemplation, https://cac.org/wp-content/uploads/2018/10/The -Bible_Lesson-4_The-Tricycle-Scripture-Experience-and-Tradition.pdf, or Pete Enns and Jared Byas, "Interview with Richard Rohr: A Contemplative Look at the Bible," *The Bible for Normal People*, podcast, March 12, 2018, https://thebible fornormalpeople.com/a-contemplative-look-at-the-bible-with-richard-rohr/.

4 "Rob Portman Commentary: Gay Couples Also Deserve Chance to Get Married," *Columbus Dispatch*, March 15, 2013, https://www.dispatch.com /story/opinion/cartoons/2013/03/15/rob-portman-commentary-gay -couples/23832285007.

Chapter 9: Quantum Weirdness

1 "Sizing Up Protons," *Nova*, The Elegant Universe, student handout, https:// www.pbs.org/wgbh/nova/teachers/activities/3012_elegant_13.html.

2 I say "roughly" because it's really only sort of halfway, but the image is still useful to help us grasp how ungraspably small the quantum level is. See "Are We Big or Small?," Physics Stack Exchange, edited July 13, 2014, https://physics .stackexchange.com/questions/44284/are-we-big-or-small. If you want to try to visualize this, see "Visualizing the Planck Length. Why Is It the Smallest Length in the Universe?" YouTube, October 12, 2019, https://www.youtube .com/watch?v=bjVfL8uNkUk.

3 Wikipedia explains Erwin Schrödinger's equation as "a linear partial differential equation that governs the wave function of a quantum-mechanical system." I'll take your word for it, Wiki. Basically, from what I can gather, the equation predicts the weird motions of subatomic particles, which can't be accounted for according to Isaac Newton's equations (which deal with the utterly predictable movements of larger objects, like planets and falling apples). Now that that's cleared up, Google "Schrödinger's cat"—unless you really love cats. "Schrödinger Equation," Wikipedia, last updated September 19, 2022, https://en.wikipedia.org/wiki/Schr%C3%B6dinger_equation.

4 See Manjit Kumar, *Quantum: Einstein, Bohr, and the Great Debate About the Nature of Reality* (London: Icon Books, 2009).

5 Not to mention space! "The first thing that can be said is we do not honestly know the true nature of space and time." Shahn Majid, "Preface," in Shahn Majid, ed., *On Space and Time* (Cambridge: Cambridge Univ. Press, 2008), ix.

6 Kelly Dickerson, "Here's Why Astronauts Age Slower Than the Rest of Us Here on Earth," Insider, August 19, 2015, https://www.businessinsider.com /do-astronauts-age-slower-than-people-on-earth-2015-8?op=1.

7 "Time Dilation," Wikipedia, last updated August 13, 2022, https://en.wikipedia .org/wiki/Time_dilation.

8 "A Roller Coaster Through Relativity/Time Dilation," Wikibooks, last modified February 16, 2018, https://en.wikibooks.org/wiki/A_Roller_Coaster _Ride_through_Relativity/Time_Dilation.

9 Carlo Rovelli, *Seven Brief Lessons on Physics* (New York: Riverhead, 2016), 60. Rovelli himself does not think the flow of time is an illusion, though Einstein at least makes room for it. On that same page, Rovelli goes on to cite a letter Einstein wrote after the death of his longtime friend Michele Besso to Besso's grieving sister: "People like us, who believe in Physics, know that the distinction made between past, present and future is nothing more than a persistent, stubborn illusion." Rovelli argues that Einstein's view of time is more complex than can be gathered from a single quotation from a private letter in a time of grief.

10 "$E = mc^2$ Explained," Einstein's Big Idea, *Nova*, August 2005, https://www .pbs.org/wgbh/nova/einstein/lrk-hand-emc2expl.html.

11 Allison, *The Luminous Dusk*, 90. I might add to Allison's list Einstein reconceiving of the universe simply by the act of thinking it through in solitude in his spare time during work hours.

12 This is true, but not entirely. It was the German physicist Max Planck who truly started the quantum revolution in 1901. Einstein did not start publishing his theories until 1905. Not a big deal in the grand scheme of things, but let's give credit where credit is due.

13 In 1964, Irish physicist John Stewart Bell worked it all out mathematically. In 1982 it was verified experimentally, and has been many times since. Sheldon Goldstein, Travis Norsen, Daniel Victor Tausk, and Nino Zanghi, "Bell's Theorem," Scholarpedia, 6(10) (2011): 8378, http://www.scholarpedia.org/article /Bell%27s_theorem. The 2022 Nobel Prize for physics was awarded to Alain Aspect, John Clauser, and Anton Zeilinger for their work in further verifying the phenomenon of quantum entanglement. https://english.elpais.com /science-tech/2022-10-18/why-quantum-entanglement-is-revolutionizing -our-understanding-of-nature.html.

14 For Bohm's words, see David Bohm, *Wholeness and the Implicate Order* (New York: Routledge, 1995). Although I cannot endorse his book as a whole, Joseph Selbie, *The Physics of God: Unifying Quantum Physics, Consciousness, M-Theory, Heaven, Neuroscience, and Transcendence* (Newburyport, MA: New Page Books, 2017), 94–97, offers a readable and, it seems to me, balanced explanation of Bohm's contribution to the question. Overall, however, the book seems to lack the grounding that a serious academic study would provide (Selbie is a yoga and meditation instructor with a modest background in undergraduate physics). The book's claim is in its subtitle. That is a tall order for anyone, and quantum physicists are generally quick to point out that one cannot simply claim that what happens in the quantum realm can be applied to anything outside of it. Having said that, I am all in favor of trying to build bridges between the science of quantum physics (and other sciences) and theology. But lines of connection have to be drawn in such a way that don't promise too much or oversimplify the science along the way.

15 I learned most of what follows from Paul Davies, *God and the New Physics* (New York: Touchstone, 1983), 107–10.

16 Davies, *God and the New Physics*, 110.

17 Physicists don't even agree on how to define "measurement" or whether it matters. See, for example, Sean Carroll, *Something Deeply Hidden: Quantum Worlds and the Emergence of Spacetime* (New York: Dutton, 2019), 17: "What exactly a measurement is, and what happens when we measure something, and what this all tells us about what's really happening behind the scenes: together, these questions constitute what's called the *measurement problem* of quantum mechanics."

Chapter 10: Quantum God-ness

1 Taylor, *The Luminous Web*, 44.
2 Delio, *The Unbearable Wholeness of Being*, 60.
3 Delio, *The Unbearable Wholeness of Being*, 15.

4 Delio, *The Unbearable Wholeness of Being*, 15. The move from Newton's "picturable and predictable" world to the quantum one is a big deal, because theology had made many intellectual accommodations to Newton's curveball. For example, God's Presence and action in the world came to be seen as supernatural *intervention* from the outside, a suspension of the cosmos that obeyed God's mechanistic rules, rather than seeing God's Presence and action woven throughout the creation. Part of what quantum physics and Process Theology open up is the ability to affirm the importance of human freedom and of divine Presence and action apart from Newton's passé view of the cosmos. Much has been written on this subject since the days of philosopher Alfred North Whitehead (1861–1947), who sought to explore the impact of the quantum revolution on the nature of meaning. Very helpful entry points to this discussion are Thomas Jay Oord, *Open and Relational Theology: An Introduction to Life-Changing Ideas* (Grasmere ID: SacraSage, 2021), and Denis Edwards, *The God of Evolution: A Trinitarian Theology* (Mahwah, NJ: Paulist, 1999).

5 For a hefty discussion of panentheism in the face of science, see Philip Clayton and Arthur Peacocke, eds., *In Whom We Live and Move and Have Our Being: Panentheistic Reflections on God's Presence in a Scientific World* (Grand Rapids, MI: Eerdmans, 2003).

6 In this respect, I have been helped by the works of Pierre Teilhard de Chardin and by two of his helpful interpreters, John F. Haught and Ilia Delio. Some of their books are listed in the bibliography.

7 Denis Edwards, *How God Acts: Creation, Redemption, and Special Divine Action* (Minneapolis, MN: Fortress, 2010), 27.

8 I am aware that the gendered language the Bible and the church have used to speak of the Trinity is a legitimate theological problem for our day and can create barriers. I hope readers will understand that in the context of this book I am simply using the conventional language because it is easily recognized. Readers are invited to employ other language, such as "Mother, Daughter, and Spirit." Along these lines, a friend passed on to me a book that includes a fascinating discussion of how some early Christian depictions of Jesus have "broad hips" that "look feminine in outline," or where "Early Christian artists have expressly given him breasts": Thomas F. Mathews, *The Clash of Gods: A Reinterpretation of Early Christian Art*, rev. ed. (Princeton, NJ: Princeton University Press), 128ff.

9 When on Easter morning Jesus tells a startled Mary Magdalene, "Do not hold on to me, because I have not yet ascended" (John 20:17), I imagine that perhaps in his transformed state Jesus was in his own interdimensional travel through space and time, where the intimate love of God for the Son conquered all barriers to relationship, death included. Musing on the mys-

tery of Easter Sunday in quantum terms is another hill I won't die on, but I don't mind letting my thoughts wander a bit, especially since I've never fully bought in to any explanation for this scene at the end of John's Gospel, nor is it clear to me what a resurrected body actually is.

10 Karl Rahner cited in Edwards, *How God Acts*, 153 (Rahner, "Dogmatic Questions on Easter," 129).

11 From St. John of Damascus's brief essay "First Apology Against Those Who Attack the Divine Images," which can be found at Aidan Kimel, "I Do Not Worship Matter, I Worship the God of Matter, Who Became Matter for My Sake," *Eclectic Orthodoxy* (blog), https://afkimel.wordpress.com/2018/02/24/i-do-not-worship-matter-i-worship-the-god-of-matter-who-became-matter-for-my-sake/.

12 The poem is "God's Grandeur."

13 Oord lays out his wonderful portrait of God as relational and relentless loving in several books, two of which are *The Uncontrolling Love of God: An Open and Relational Control of Providence* (Downers Grove, IL: IVP Academic, 2015), and *Pluriform Love: An Open and Relational Theology of Well-Being* (Grasmere, ID: SacraSage, 2022).

Chapter 11: Thin Places

1 Taylor, *The Luminous Web*, 54. Carlo Rovelli, *Helgoland: Making Sense of the Quantum Revolution* (New York: Riverhead, 2021), tells of a friend's similar experience: "My good friend Lee recounts that as a young man he lay on his bed for hours on end looking at the ceiling, after he had studied entanglement. He was thinking about how each atom in his body must have interacted in some distant past with so many other atoms in the universe. Every atom in his body had to be entangled with billions of atoms dispersed throughout the galaxy . . . He felt a connectedness with the cosmos."

2 This is a major theme in N. T. Wright, *Surprised by Hope: Rethinking Heaven, the Resurrection, and the Mission of the Church* (San Francisco: HarperOne, 2008).

3 Dale C. Allison, *Night Comes: Death, Imagination, and the Last Things* (Grand Rapids, MI: Eerdmans, 2016), 36.

4 "Is There Life After Death? Fifty Years of Research at UVA," YouTube, February 22, 2017, https://www.youtube.com/watch?v=0AtTM9hgCDw&t=2362s. For a deeper dive into the research, a good place to start is Janice Miner Holden, Bruce Greyson, and Debbie James, eds., *The Handbook of Near-Death Experiences: Thirty Years of Investigation* (Santa Barbara, CA: Praeger, 2009), and John C. Hagen III, ed., *The Science of Near-Death Experiences* (Columbia: University of Missouri Press).

5 Bruce Greyson, "I Study NDEs. What I Learned About Near-Death Experiences Changed My Life," *Newsweek*, March 13, 2021, https://www.newsweek.com/i-worked-people-who-came-back-brink-death-1575676.

6 Bruce Leininger and Andrea Leininger, *Soul Survivor: The Reincarnation of a World War II Fighter Pilot* (New York: Grand Central Publishing, 2009).

7 I recommend highly Allison, *Night Comes*, Dale C. Allison Jr., *Embracing Mystery: Religious Experience in a Secular Age* (Grand Rapids, MI: Eerdmans, 2022), and part 3 of the massive Dale C. Allison Jr., *The Resurrection of Jesus: Apologetics, Polemics, History* (London: T&T Clark, 2021).

8 Allison, *Night Comes*, 14–15.

9 "Greyson NDE Scale," IANDS, last updated June 11, 2022, https://iands.org/research/nde-research/important-research-articles/698-greyson-nde-scale.html.

10 Caleb Wilde, *All the Ways Our Dead Still Speak: A Funeral Director on Life, Death, and the Hereafter* (Minneapolis, MN: Broadleaf, 2022), 24.

11 Molly's story, as well as information on the Molly Steinsapir Foundation, can be found at https://mollysteinsapir.com.

12 Bradley Jersak, *Her Gates Will Never Be Shut: Hope, Hell, and the New Jerusalem* (Eugene, OR: Wipf & Stock, 2009), 120–21. Jersak cites the third-century theologian Origen, *De Principiis* 1.1.1, found in *Ancient Nicene Fathers*, Vol. 4. See also Hans Urs von Balthazar, *Dare We Hope "That All Men Be Saved"?*, 2nd ed. (San Francisco: Ignatius Press, 2014); Gregory MacDonald, *The Evangelical Universalist: A Biblical Hope That God's Love Will Save All*, 2nd ed. (Eugene, OR: Cascade, 2012); Bradley Jersak, *A More Christlike God: A More Beautiful Gospel* (Pasadena, CA: CWRpress, 2015).

13 I say "similar" because this episode also has dwarves who refuse to fully enter the real Narnia and receive what Aslan wants to give them. This suggests that Lewis is more of an inclusivist than universalist.

14 Teilhard calls this future the "omega point" (omega being the last letter of the Greek alphabet). See John F. Haught, *The Cosmic Vision of Teihard de Chardin* (Maryknoll, NY: Orbis, 2021), 17–33.

15 Recently, Richard Rohr has described his own understanding of this dimension in *The Universal Christ: How a Forgotten Reality Can Change Everything We See, Hope for, and Believe* (New York: Convergent, 2019).

16 Shout-out to the 1960s and Crosby, Stills, Nash, and Young's version of Joni Mitchell's classic song "Woodstock."

17 George L. Murphy works out this idea in *The Cosmos in Light of the Cross* (Harrisburg, PA: Trinity Press, 2003).

18 Richard Beck, *The Slavery of Death* (Eugene, OR: Cascade, 2014), 31.

19 Einstein quoted in Allison, *The Resurrection of Jesus*, 358–59 (from Einstein and Infeld, *Evolution of Physics*, 31).

Chapter 12: Catching Glimpses

1 I am grateful for my colleague of ten years, theologian Dr. Eric Flett, for continually encouraging me to engage the implications of global Christianity.

2 I have learned much from Bessel A. van der Kolk, *The Body Keeps the Score: Brain, Mind, and Body in the Healing of Trauma* (New York: Viking, 2014).

3 Thomas Keating, *Invitation to Love: The Way of Christian Contemplation* (New York: Continuum, 2007), defines "divine therapy" as "a paradigm in which the spiritual journey is presented as a form of psychotherapy designed to heal the emotional wounds of early childhood and our mechanisms for coping with them." More briefly, see Thomas Keating, *The Human Condition: Contemplation and Transformation* (New York: Paulist, 1999), 29–45; see also Kyriacos C. Markides, *Gifts of the Desert: The Forgotten Path of Christian Spirituality* (New York: Doubleday, 2005).

4 See the opening chapter in John Calvin's *Institutes of the Christian Religion* ("The Connection Between the Knowledge of God and the Knowledge of Ourselves"), which is available in various editions and formats. An online version can be found at Project Gutenberg, https://www.gutenberg.org /files/45001/45001-h/45001-h.htm: "True and substantial wisdom principally consists of two parts, the knowledge of God, and the knowledge of ourselves. But, while these two branches of knowledge are so intimately connected, which of them precedes and produces the other, is not easy to discover. For, in the first place, no man can take a survey of himself but he must immediately turn to the contemplation of God, in whom he 'lives and moves'; . . . On the other hand, it is plain that no man can arrive at the true knowledge of himself, without having first contemplated the divine character, and then descended to the consideration of his own" (Chapter 1, Sections 1 and 2).

5 Hart, *The Experience of God*, 44.

Bibliography

I normally don't like flooding readers with a long bibliography, as if I'm giving homework or something, but this is a different kind of book for me to write. I had to (better, *got* to) do a lot of reading outside of my usual areas—namely, science—and I want you to know what I've been reading. I've whittled the list down to books I have actually cited and some others (mainly in the science category) that I have benefitted from more generally, that are for the most part quite readable, and that I wanted to share with you. Internet sources are not included here but can be found in the endnotes.

Allison, Dale C., Jr. *Embracing Mystery: Religious Experience in a Secular Age.* Grand Rapids, MI: Eerdmans, 2022.

———. *The Luminous Dusk: Finding God in the Deep, Still Places.* Grand Rapids, MI: Eerdmans, 2006.

———. *Night Comes: Death, Imagination, and the Last Things.* Grand Rapids, MI: Eerdmans, 2016.

———. *The Resurrection of Jesus: Apologetics, Polemics, History.* London: T&T Clark, 2021.

St. Augustine. *The Literal Meaning of Genesis.* Translated by J. H. Taylor. 2 vols. New York: Paulist, 1982.

Balthazar, Hans Urs von. *Dare We Hope "That All Men Be Saved"?* 2nd ed. San Francisco: Ignatius Press, 2014.

Beck, Richard. *The Slavery of Death.* Eugene, OR: Cascade, 2014.

Becker, Adam. *What Is Real?: The Unfinished Quest for the Meaning of Quantum Physics*. New York: Basic, 2018.

Bell, Rob. *What We Talk About When We Talk About God*. San Francisco: HarperOne, 2013.

Bembenek, Scott. *The Cosmic Machine: The Science That Runs Our Universe and the Story Behind It*. San Diego: Zoari, 2017.

Bohm, David. *Wholeness and the Implicate Order*. New York: Routledge, 1995.

Brown, William P. *The Seven Pillars of Creation: The Bible, Science, and the Ecology of Wonder*. Oxford: Oxford Univ. Press, 2010.

Byas, Jared. *Love Matters More: How Fighting to Be Right Keeps Us from Loving like Jesus*. Grand Rapids, MI: Zondervan, 2020.

Carroll, Sean. *Something Deeply Hidden: Quantum Worlds and the Emergence of Spacetime*. New York: Dutton, 2019.

Case-Winters, Anna. *God Will Be All in All: Theology Through the Lens of Incarnation*. Louisville, KY: Westminster John Knox, 2021.

Clayton, Philip and Arthur Peacocke, eds. *In Whom We Live and Move and Have Our Being: Panentheistic Reflections on God's Presence in a Scientific World*. Grand Rapids, MI: Eerdmans, 2003.

Davies, Paul. *God and the New Physics*. New York: Touchstone, 1983.

Delio, Ilia. *The Unbearable Wholeness of Being: God, Evolution, and the Power of Love*. Maryknoll, NY: Orbis, 2013.

Edwards, Denis. *The God of Evolution: A Trinitarian Theology*. Mahwah, NJ: Paulist, 1999.

———. *How God Acts: Creation, Redemption, and Special Divine Action*. Minneapolis: Fortress, 2010.

Einstein, Albert, and Leopold Infeld. *The Evolution of Physics from Early Concepts of Relativity and Quanta*. New York: Simon & Schuster, 1996 (1938).

Enns, Peter. *The Bible Tells Me So: Why Defending Scripture Has Made Us Unable to Read It*. San Francisco: HarperOne, 2014.

———. *The Evolution of Adam: What the Bible Does and Doesn't Say About Human Origins*. 10th anniversary ed. Grand Rapids, MI: Baker, 2022.

————. *How the Bible Actually Works: In Which I Explain How an Ancient, Ambiguous, and Diverse Book Leads Us to Wisdom Rather Than Answers— and Why That's Good News.* San Francisco: HarperOne, 2019.

————. *Inspiration and Incarnation: Evangelicals and the Problem of the Old Testament.* 10th anniversary ed. Grand Rapids, MI: Baker, 2015.

————. *The Sin of Certainty: Why God Desires Our Trust More Than Our "Correct" Beliefs.* San Francisco: HarperOne, 2016.

Greene, Brian. *The Elegant Universe: Superstrings, Hidden Dimensions, and the Quest for the Ultimate Theory.* 2nd ed. New York: Norton, 2011.

————. *The Fabric of the Cosmos: Space, Time, and the Texture of Reality.* New York: Vintage, 2005.

Hagen, John C. III, ed. *The Science of Near-Death Experiences.* Columbia: Univ. of Missouri Press, 2017.

Hart, David Bentley. *The Experience of God: Being, Consciousness, Bliss.* New Haven, CT: Yale Univ. Press, 2013.

————. *That All Shall Be Saved: Heaven, Hell, and Universal Salvation.* New Haven, CT: Yale Univ. Press, 2019.

Haught, John F. *The Cosmic Vision of Teilhard de Chardin.* Maryknoll, NY: Orbis, 2021.

Holden, Janice Miner, Bruce Greyson, and Debbie James, eds. *The Handbook of Near-Death Experiences: Thirty Years of Investigation.* Santa Barbara, CA: Praeger, 2009.

Jersak, Bradley. *Her Gates Will Never Be Shut: Hope, Hell, and the New Jerusalem.* Eugene, OR: Wipf & Stock, 2009.

————. *A More Christlike God: A More Beautiful Gospel.* Pasadena, CA: CWRpress, 2015.

Kaiser, David. *How the Hippies Saved Physics: Science, Counterculture, and the Quantum Revival.* New York: Norton, 2011.

Keating, Thomas. *The Human Condition: Contemplation and Transformation.* New York: Paulist, 1999.

————. *Invitation to Love: The Way of Christian Contemplation.* New York: Continuum, 2007.

Kolk, Bessel A. van der. *The Body Keeps the Score: Brain, Mind, and Body in the Healing of Trauma*. New York: Viking, 2014.

Kugel, James L. *The Great Shift: Encountering God in Biblical Times*. Boston: Houghton Mifflin, 2017.

———. *How to Read the Bible*. New York: Free Press, 2007.

Kumar, Manjit. *Quantum: Einstein, Bohr, and the Great Debate About the Nature of Reality*. London: Icon Books, 2009.

Lamoureux, Denis O. *Evolution: Scripture and Nature Say Yes*. Grand Rapids, MI: Zondervan, 2016.

———. *Evolutionary Creation: A Christian Approach to Evolution*. Eugene, OR: Wipf & Stock, 2008.

———. *I Love Jesus and I Accept Evolution*. Eugene, OR: Wipf & Stock, 2009.

Leininger, Bruce and Andrea Leininger. *Soul Survivor: The Reincarnation of a World War II Fighter Pilot*. New York: Grand Central Publishing, 2009.

Levenson, Jon D. *Creation and the Persistence of Evil: The Jewish Drama of Divine Omnipotence*. San Francisco: HarperOne, 1988.

———. *Love of God: Divine Gift, Human Gratitude, and Mutual Faithfulness in Judaism*. Princeton, NJ: Princeton Univ. Press, 2016.

Lewis, C. S. *The Chronciles of Narnia*. San Francisco, CA: HarperCollins, 1994.

———. *Mere Christianity*. London: Macmillan, 1952.

Lightman, Alan. *Probably Impossibilities: Musings on Beginnings and Endings*. New York: Vintage, 2022.

Lombard, Jay. *The Mind of God: Neuroscience, Faith, and a Search for the Soul*. New York: Harmony, 2017.

MacDonald, Gregory. *The Evangelical Universalist: A Biblical Hope That God's Love Will Save All*. 2nd ed. Eugene, OR: Cascade, 2012.

Majid, Shahn. "Preface." In *On Space and Time*, edited by Shahn Majid, xi–xx. Cambridge: Cambridge Univ. Press, 2008.

Markides, Kyriacos C. *Gifts of the Desert: The Forgotten Path of Christian Spirituality*. New York: Doubleday, 2005.

Mathews, Thomas F. *The Clash of Gods: A Reinterpretation of Early Christian Art*. Rev. ed. Princeton, NJ: Princeton Univ. Press, 1999.

McHargue, Mike. *Finding God in the Waves: How I Lost My Faith and Found It Again Through Science*. New York: Convergent, 2016.

Miller, Keith B., ed. *Perspectives on an Evolving Creation*. Grand Rapids, MI: Eerdmans, 2003.

Murphy, George L. *The Cosmos in Light of the Cross*. Harrisburg, PA: Trinity Press International, 2003.

O'Murchu, Diarmuid. *Quantum Theology: Spiritual Implications of the New Physics*. Spring Valley, NY: Crossroad, 1997.

Oord, Thomas Jay. *Open and Relational Theology: An Introduction to Life-Changing Ideas*. Grasmere, ID: SacraSage, 2021.

———. *Pluriform Love: An Open and Relational Theology of Well-Being*. Grasmere, ID: SacraSage, 2022.

———. *The Uncontrolling Love of God: An Open and Relational Control of Providence*. Downers Grove, IL: IVP Academic, 2015.

Panek, Richard. *Dark Matter, Dark Energy, and the Race to Discover the Rest of Reality*. Boston: Mariner, 2011.

Pascal, Blaise. *Pensées*. Translated by W. F. Trotter. Available at Christian Classics Ethereal Library, https://ccel.org/ccel/pascal/pensees/pensees.

Polkinghorne, John. *Exploring Reality: The Intertwining of Science and Religion*. New Haven, CT: Yale Univ. Press, 2005.

———. *Quantum Physics and Theology*. New Haven, CT: Yale Univ. Press, 2007.

———. *Quarks, Chaos and Christianity: Questions to Science and Religion*. Spring Valley, NY: Crossroad, 2006.

Rahner, Karl. "Dogmatic Questions on Easter." In *Theological Investigations. Vol. 4: More Recent Writings*, translated by Kevin Smyth, 121–33. London: Darton, Longman & Todd, 1974.

———. *Foundations of Christian Faith: An Introduction to the Idea of Christianity*. New York: Seabury, 1978.

———. "The Spirituality of the Church of the Future." In *Theological Investigations. Vol. 20: Concern for the Church*, translated by Edward Quinn, 143–53. New York: Crossroad, 1981.

Ratzinger, Joseph. *Jesus of Nazareth: From the Baptism in the Jordan to the Transfiguration*. Translated by Adrian J. Walker. New York: Doubleday, 2007.

Raymo, Chet. *The Soul of the Night: An Astronomical Pilgrimage*. Cambridge, MA: Cowley, 1992.

Rendsburg, Gary A. "The Genesis of the Bible." Inaugural lecture, October 28, 2004. https://jewishstudies.rutgers.edu/docman/rendsburg/117-the-genesis-of-the-bible/file.

———. *How the Bible Is Written*. Peabody, MA: Hendrickson, 2019.

Rohr, Richard. *The Universal Christ: How a Forgotten Reality Can Change Everything We See, Hope for, and Believe*. New York: Convergent, 2019.

Ross, Elisabeth Kübler. *On Life After Death*. Berkeley: Celestial Books, 2008.

Rovelli, Carlo. *Helgoland: Making Sense of the Quantum Revolution*. New York: Riverhead, 2021.

———. *The Order of Time*. New York: Riverhead, 2018.

———. *Reality Is Not What It Seems: The Journey to Quantum Gravity*. New York: Riverhead, 2017.

———. *Seven Brief Lessons on Physics*. New York: Riverhead, 2016.

Russell, John Robert, gen. ed. *Scientific Perspectives on Divine Action*. 5 volumes. Vatican City State: Vatican Observatory Publications/Berkeley, CA: Center for Theology and Natural Sciences, 1993–2001.

Sacks, Jonathan. *The Great Partnership: Science, Religion, and the Search for Meaning*. New York: Schocken, 2011.

Scharf, Caleb. *The Zoomable Universe: An Epic Tour Through Cosmic Scale, from Almost Everything to Nearly Nothing*. New York: Scientific American/Farrar, Straus and Giroux, 2017.

Sommer, Benjamin D. *Revelation and Authority: Sinai in Jewish Scripture and Tradition*. New Haven, CT: Yale Univ. Press, 2016.

Stanich, Roland Michael. *Integral Christianity: The Way of Embodied Love*. Bright Alliance, 2021.

Taylor, Barbara Brown. *Learning to Walk in the Dark*. San Francisco: HarperOne, 2014.

————. *The Luminous Web: Faith, Science and the Experience of Wonder.* London: Canterbury, 2000.

Teilhard de Chardin, Pierre. *Christianity and Evolution.* New York: Harcourt, 1971.

————. *The Future of Man.* New York: Harper & Row, 1964.

Todd, Peter B. *The Individuation of God: Integrating Science and Religion.* Asheville, NC: Chiron, 2017.

Wilde, Caleb. *All the Ways Our Dead Still Speak: A Funeral Director on Life, Death, and the Hereafter.* Minneapolis: Broadleaf, 2022.

Worthing, Mark William. *God, Creation and Contemporary Physics.* Minneapolis: Fortress, 1996.

Wright, N. T. *Surprised by Hope: Rethinking Heaven, the Resurrection, and the Mission of the Church.* San Francisco: HarperOne, 2008.

Zohar, Danah. *The Quantum Self: Human Nature and Consciousness Defined by the New Physics.* New York: HarperCollins, 1990.